THE CONDITION

OF THE

BLACKMAN

A 21st CENTURY ANALYSIS

ABDUL-MALIK MASOKA

CLASSIC AGE PUBLISHING

Classic Age Publishing,

271 Kent Avenue,

Randburg

South Africa

2191

www.classicagepublishing.co.za

Proofread and edited by : Dr Steella of Excellent Proofreaders

Book and Cover design by : Ghalluh

Layout and typesetting by : Vukulu Sizwe Maphindani

ISBN: 978-0-9947069-9-7

Also available as an e-book.

First Published in 2015 by Dots & Pixels Media and Publishing.

CONTENTS

DEDICATION & AKNOWLEDGEMENTS................. 1

INTRODUCTION... 6

CHAPTER 1: My Baby Brother 16

CHAPTER 2: My Teenage Brother 25

CHAPTER 4: My White-Collar Brother 46

CHAPTER 5: My Intergrated Brother.......................... 54

CHAPTER 6: My Christian Brother............................. 74

CHAPTER 7: My political Brother 92

CHAPTER 8: My Millitary Brother 125

CHAPTER 9: My Celebrity Brother........................... 149

CHAPTER 10: In Conclusion: A Solution By A
Blackman.. 161

ABOUT THE BOOK 243

DEDICATION &
AKNOWLEDGEMENTS

This I must make very clear; this book is for anybody but not for everybody. This work is for thinking Black Men, not the happy-go-lucky. I have seen, in the past and present, true Black leaders being ridiculed, verbally attacked and assaulted by the very same people they fight for and represent, and this would hurt me deeply, thinking to myself; I don't want to go through this, knowing very well I've already set myself up for it. Therefore, those of you, my beloved Brothers, who are not deep in thought, who never make time to read scriptures and study religion, make time to brainstorm politics, ancient philosophy and intellectual issues and ideas; this book isn't for you – until you do so. This book is not dedicated to the satisfied, the isolated, the full and happy; it is not for those who say, "it's all good" because it's not all good! It is rather for the secluded, the empty and unsatisfied; those who believe this is not how things were meant to be. Those who believe that we should improve; we should go further, we should learn more, teach more, and live more. This is for the one who says aloud "In the Name of God, with Truth, I will fight for Justice until the end".

I dedicate this book to the ones who have found 'Brotherhood in Blackness', the ones who believe that God is the Almighty, and the ones who are seeking God through Knowledge of Self, the ones who believe that Afrika is rich in nature, as are Afrikans. This is for the ones who see no racial superiority in the above statement, rather racial acknowledgment born of self-realization and racial consciousness, which is a birth-right given to all of mankind.

To my Mother; my guardian angel, my earth and my paradise, and my Father, my Grandparents, my Wife and my Daughter. To my Aunts, Uncles, Grandaunts and Granduncles. My Cousins. My Brothers; Simphiwe Mbhele, my younger Brother Luthando Mngomezulu, Edwin Thabile Dlomo, Siyabonga Siwundla, Sbusiso Kheswa and Monwabisi Nzipazi. These are intelligent young Black men who inspire me by challenging me every day, always pushing my way of thinking to higher heights. My uncles and teachers Wanda Hlatshwayo and Xolani Hlatshwayo, my elder Brother Sbusiso Masoka and younger Brother Njabulo Masoka, not forgetting my Beautiful Sisters. This is for my late grandmother, Joyce maHlatshwayo-Vezi, a very pious Christian woman who gave me my first copy of the Glorious Koran back in 2005 which I have read ever since. May Allah reward you, thank you for giving me dawah (invitation to the right path). May each word I ever read and continue to read count as ten blessings for you, ameen. I dedicate this work to my late uncle and friend, Thamsanqa "Tsopi" Hlatshwayo, your passing broke me down and tore me apart, nothing will ever be the same without you. I pay honor to my Spiritual Father and Righteous Teacher, ungikhulisile Baba, wangakha, The Honorable Minister Adam Tembelani Mbhele ka Ncanywa and his committee; Community of Believers and ACASDOOSA (AbaNgoni Cultural and Skills Development Organization of South Africa), and his late friend, Brother, and colleague, Master Umar Moleleki. My guiding elder Al-Hajji Hamza Mbhele, may Allah be pleased with you, I love you for the sake of Allah. Another guiding elder of mine, Sheikh Cele of Marianhill, may Allah preserve you. Peace to my Brother Zaid Muslim of Umlazi. My salutation and respect goes to the man who polished this work, my new friend Dr. Richard

Steele. I dedicate this work to the Brothers I grew up with and those I met along the way. I dedicate this book to my family and friends, my Facebook, Twitter, and Tumblr family, I regard you as real friends and family. This project is dedicated to my close and distant Black Brothers all over the world, and my Brothers in faith. My Sudanese Brothers Osman, Imam Omary Joseph Sekamana, my Brother Salaam Ngcobo, my guardian Brother Ibrahiem Mthembu, you are the most supreme example of a Muslim character that I've ever met. This is for the inspirational leaders I came to know about: Maulana Ishmiel Patel – thank you for Jummah talks in Jummah Masjid, Grey Street, Durban; Maulana Ahmad Kathrada of Darul Ihsan Islamic Services Centre and colleague Maulana Sabir Ibrahiem; the late Dawood Ngwane (inna lillahi wa anna alayhi rajioon), author of Ubhaqa (The Light), the one book I believe is the greatest ever written for the South Afrikan so-called non-Muslim Black man; my Teachers' Teacher, the late great Sheikh Ahmed Deedat (inna lillahi wa anna alayhi rajioon) of IPCI (Islamic Propagation Centre International) and all members and workers of IPCI. With this work I pay homage to the Lamontville Muslim movement, probably the earliest Muslim establishment in KZN townships. This is for the members and offspring of The Ikwantu Muslim Society, an organization of Muslims of

Afrikan origin (Inanda-KwaMashu-Ntuzuma) formed in 1977. I dedicate this to the believers and preachers of Peace (Ukuthula) from all world religions, known and unknown. This is for the victims of human engineered poverty and diseases; this is for the laborers – the builders of roads, tourist attractions, schools, and hospitals – grand architects; this is for my blue-collar Brothers.

After all is said and done, and after all the fights and arguments, I desperately hope that in my writings you do not find hatred, resentment and anger, for there is none. I hope you see love, compassion and solidarity.

INTRODUCTION

This is a call of Unity

I am who I am. Truth is my Shepherd. When the Voice of Truth calls, I follow. I humble myself and follow in her footsteps. I trust the Voice – how can I not, when it comes through within me, but not from me; from the Creator, the All-Knowing. In each of us, the Voice utters the very same Message, with the very same tone, in the very same pitch. The Voice is inside each human. Some of us hear the Voice clearly and we call these people 'crazy'. Some hear it from a distance, and we call them 'skeptics'. And the rest do not hear the Voice – and those are the dead among us, we call them 'normal'.

D-evil man is wickedly wise. In order to keep us

destructed from hearing the Message, while keeping us spiritually corrupted, he has given us 24 hour 'entertainment'. He gives us thousands of different sports, billions of corny music tracks, restaurants to serve us deadly foods genetically modified, bars for brain-damaging beverages, internet, social websites, corny movies, and corny television shows, all to destruct and mislead me and you with this bunch of junk we think we enjoy, called entertainment. Brother Malcolm X heard this Voice, and he spoke to us untremblingly through the Voice of the Creator. This is why his message lives. So did Patrice Lumumba, Robert Sobukwe, George Jackson, and many others, and this is solely why we hold them dearly, close to our hearts. There is an uncompromising distinction: my spirit, by the Creator's will, does not heed to my body, rather my body heeds to my spirit. This is the first step to being whole, wholly or holy (Ukupheleliswa ngobungcwele). Nevertheless, remember, being holy has got less to do with being spiritual and more to do with being knowledgeable. This is not to say that men are born unspiritual, it is actually the opposite. Then again, knowledge is required for one to become conscious of one's spiritual self. Knowledge is required for one to become aware of the Creator's existence because the Creator is seen through Creation (not sight of the naked eye), in everyone and everything. Knowledge is required for one to realize that the Creator lives in him, and in all of us. This re-ally-zation is truly a re-ligion; it is to legion again, as you and the Creator were before the destruction of Adam and the Adamites.

Ignorance of Self is what separates us from the Creator. Moreover, when we are separated from the Creator, we think independently, therefore act likewise. Whenever I do well, it is because I was doing that with All-Mighty God Allah, but when I do badly, it is because I was acting all by myself. It is my fault. Even so ignorance is what separates us from uMvelinqangi, remember, my beloved Brothers and Sisters: ignorance is not the lack of knowledge, it is the lack of realization that you do know. Therefore, the first step to acquiring some knowledge is to realize that you are not a fool, you are not dumb, and you do not lack anything, all the answers are in you and all around you. The answers concerning life are in life itself. No one can teach men anything, we can only help each other remember (what we already know) and then re-ligion with ourselves and all of Creation, which is the only way to re-ligion with the Creator. This is not some sort of self-worship, rather a God-search through Knowledge of Self. Allah said 'We made your body a temple, and We lived there', in the Bible God says, "I don't dwell in the temples made by the hands of men". YOU are holy!

In order to get relevant answers, there are relevant questions that need to be asked. And when those answers are found, they will have to be examined and thoroughly challenged until we prove them undeniable.

As highly quoted as this book is, it is, however, not for inspiration. I have no intention or desire to inspire anyone. It is meant to share the Truth as I see it (not as how it is). Inspirational words are nothing more than a glass of water to the depressed, the spiritually thirsty. Motivational speakers and motivational writers are nothing more than a water tap. They draw their knowledge from the well of Truth, for the Truth is the well of life. But, there is something Greater than the well – the Rain, which is where all the waters of life come from, the Source of all Knowledge – The Creator. Remember, the rain falls on every man's house, but it is left to each man to go find the well when there is no rain. Likewise, Allah is in every man's heart, but it is left to each man to search for Allah. We usually listen to inspirational speakers on our radios, watch them on our televisions, read their words in magazines, and hear them in our churches, and we are moved by these creative talks, but inspiration does not last, nor does bathing and a sweet smell. If you have a water tap, each time I become thirsty I will knock on your door for a glass of water. I will become dependent on you, my survival will rest in your hands. Motivational speakers are unintentionally selfish. If a man is hungry, free him, emancipate him, for hunger and thirst are biological forms of slavery. If a man comes to you hungry, do not give him fish and let him go, soon he will come back when the fish is finished, and if you don't feed him again he will stick a gun in your face and rob you of your fish. Give him a rod and bait and show him the river. If a man comes to you thirsty, don't just give him a glass of water, take him to the well. All of us are in pain, and we all need help. If a man comes to you depressed, do not motivate him, to motivate is to cheer up. Tell him the Truth, it will hurt him but it will also free him and lead him to the Creator, the Superior Source of All Knowledge. Truth is de-motivational; in fact, it brings sorrow, it brings tears, but it is these tears that wash your eyes, your deluded sight so that you can see clearly. If your eyes have not been washed by the tears of Truth, everything you see is a Lie; for you see life through contaminated lenses. We are limited beings, limited by our physical bodies and material desires, until we master these so-called limitations, we can truly become Gods again like we were once upon a time. You may be asking yourself why I keep on saying 'The Truth', instead of 'A Truth'. The Creator is One, but can be understood in many different ways, but it is the same Creator – so is the Truth. I write this book in desperate hope that it will open our eyes that have been blinded by lies and propaganda. I hope this book will help us grow, and learn to see the Creator within us and in everyone and everything. But, I cannot hold your hand and lead you before the 'Throne' of the Almighty, not even your own father can do that for you. I do not have that authority, nor the ability. Only the Truth has such authority and power, for the Truth is pure – I am not. However, I can lead you to the Truth and leave you at the 'gate', and then the Truth itself will lead you to the Almighty, for Truth is Light, therefore follow in Her footprints. The Truth is the bridge between Man and his Creator. Those among us who have journeyed through the path of Truth are truly One with the Creator. There is no space between us, the bridge has vanished, and we cannot look back or forwards for there is nothing to remember, and there is nothing to contemplate. There is only the now. Without being apologetic, I have to remind you that this is not a religious book either. However, we cannot separate Man and Belief, Faith, or Religion, because all of mans' condition is caused either by Belief or by the lack of Belief. This book is dedicated to my People, my Black Brothers and Sisters. The Condition of the Black Man is intended to bring the Black Man back to Himself, and therefore back to the Creator. The focus is on the Black man simply because he is the most strayed, most targeted, most lied to, and the one with most life span. However, this book, more than anything, is about Understanding. It is also about Compassion and Love. Compassion and Love are parents to Insight. He who has no compassion and love cannot obtain any knowledge, nor insight, therefore will forever remain a stranger to Wisdom, for Wisdom is a reward of love and compassion to the loving and compassionate. It is not a gift – it is a reward. 'Gift' is an understatement, for 'gift' is some sort of charity but 'reward' is born of justice, it can only be earned.

Before a man is born, he is not non-existent, he exists in spirit. He is One with the Creator. His birth gives him flesh and that flesh separates him from the Almighty, but he does not lose his spiritual self, which is what keeps him connected with his Maker. However, because of the flesh, he is now not fully connected with the Creator though his spirituality is fully aware of the Creator but struggles with the flesh which can be understood as his 'weaker Self' or 'lower Self', for it is vulnerable to temptations, desires, diseases, and the flesh ultimately and eventually dies. The spirit serves as a man's reminder of the Most High and it yearns for that Supreme reunion. This yearning is to be fed food of the spirit, food of the soul until it is stabilized. It should not be full, for there has to be a balance between the spiritual and the material. That which is stable is even and still, but that which is full is crippled and corrupted.

The fact of the matter is that we are at war, and everyone is involved in this war; some are aware of this phenomenon, most are not. But we are all part of this Great War. The Black man's condition is not geographical, that would be undermining the Black man's struggle. The fact of the matter is that the Black man's condition is universal; there is a global conspiracy against the Black man, which is why there is a great need for all Black men around the globe to unite, now more than ever – spiritually, consciously, economically, socially, and even physically. We must maintain physical contact too, we must bridge this social gap between us, we must visit each other, cross the road, the lake, river, even the ocean, just to visit our Black Brother from another place or country.

Black people of this world are very much misled through religion and politics, and now we've found ourselves caught up in this super-sized belly of the beast. How did we end up here? Who is the Beast? And how can we get out? These are the questions we are going to examine and solve, God Willing. Our great God-given Understanding of Life was snatched from us by man-made religions and false politics and was replaced by blind faith and fear. The Black man will not heal until he examines and understands the origin, cause and effect of his plight. His freedom will remain a fairytale until he learns of his true history and accepts it as it is. His mentality has been thoroughly contaminated, and for so long, that he is hardly able to shake off the white view of himself, which is self-inferior and self-sub-serving.

After reading this book, God Willing, we will understand what brought us where we currently are, mentally, biologically, economically, socially, and spiritually. This book is based on my research findings and my personal analysis, therefore, I am not looking for compliments, I'm looking for constructive critique and debate. Despite all the criticisms, arguments, and punches that may be thrown and portrayed in this book towards my Brethren, this is a call for unity. UNITED WE STRIVE, DIVIDED WE PERISH!

May we stay constantly reminded that it's all about Love

and it's all about the People.

We will lead the revolution!

May God the Almighty bless this union as I welcome you to Umsamo;

I greet you with a Universal Revolutionary Salutation of Peace and Solidarity: As-Salaam Alaikum! In the Zulu language we say, "Ukuthula Makube Nawe".

"I do not come with timeless truths.

My consciousness is not illuminated with ultimate radiances. Nevertheless, in complete composure, I think it would be good if certain things were said."
– Frantz Fanon

CHAPTER 1

MY BABY BROTHER

No matter what it takes, our children have to march forth

I remember being a little boy growing up in a Christian home in a Christian dominated Black neighborhood called *Lamont Native Village*, affectionately known as *Lamontville*, named after a then Mayor of Durban, *Reverend Archibald Lamont*, probably a Caucasian Christian missionary. Living in a full house with uncles, aunts and cousins, I remember that my beautiful young mother – the very first woman I loved, trusted, and submitted to, my first and greatest teacher – would occasionally tell me to squeeze my nose when I wake up in the morning and she never told me why nor did I ever ask. But maybe, just maybe, as I once heard from a Black female colleague, a sharp nose in a man symbolizes that he is *easy-going* and *understanding*, while a flat nose (like the Black man's nose, my nose) indicates that he is *insensitive* and *hard-headed*. Therefore, the sharp-nose, like the white man's nose, is beautiful and good, and the flat nose is ugly and bad.

I remember women in my extended family wearing wigs, perms, or straightening their naturally beautiful tangled hair, so that it would look like white women's hair. I remember the dark-skinned women in my neighborhood wearing make-up and using all sorts of facial creams to bleach their beautiful dark skin so that it would become light like a white woman's skin. I remember light-skinned Black girls getting all kinds of lovely compliments and receiving undeserved favors, even from strangers. And I remember the dark-skinned ones being called '*mubi*' (ugly), and being called all kinds of derogatory names – 'monkey', 'baboon', '*mnyamana*' ('blackie' with a negative connotation), etc. I also remember the light-skinned girl being called '*intombi yoMlungu*' (white lady), and being told she looks like an 'Angel'. I remember parents treating their own children differently due to 'good' or 'bad' looks which was generally determined by their skin complexion. If a child was lighter compared to the others, they were treated differently. I vividly remember girls popularly known by their English names generally perceived as having good-looks, even if they did not. Now that I have grown wiser, I have realized the fact that we all suffered from mental poisoning which conditioned our young minds, concurrently creating both optical illusion and mental delusion which beautifies everything that is closest to whiteness and white character; light skin, straight hair, European names.

Growing up in a Christian environment, I remember myself and my cousins and close friends going to *Sunday School* every Sunday morning and being told that angels wear white clothes and that in order to go to heaven our hearts must remain pure as 'white'. I remember the painting of *The Last Supper* by *Leonardo Da Vinci* in every other home in my neighborhood, hanging on the walls, and I remember noticing that the man we were taught to pray to, the name to call upon whenever in need, *Jesus Christ*, and all his disciples, were white people. From the Bible story books we read, to the television stories we watched – all were populated by white people. I remember going to clinics and hospitals and noticing that Blacks were nurses and whites were doctors. I remember that company bosses were white, general workers Black. I recall being fully convinced that police officers, nurses, teachers, must be Black, and entrepreneurs, doctors, lawyers, must be white. Even up to a later age, when I saw a white schoolteacher, in the back of my mind I screamed *'loser!'*. I saw a white individual who failed in life, someone who was destined to be a lawyer or doctor but ended up being a teacher. By the same token, when I saw a Black schoolteacher, I paid homage. I saw a hero, a successful Brother or Sister; a role model. I remember my young naïve self convinced that all prisoners are Black, all pilots are white. Now, imagine what self-image I had as a Black child. And I was no exception. It hurts me to look back in remembrance of all these things. It hurts me because that which I call 'yesterday' is our children's 'today', that which is to me a memory is to them the 'here and now'. It hurts me because to me this rusty reality is to them a glittery one. I see a false history, they see a true Age. I have been purposely derailed from the trail of life and thrown into the abyss. By the will of God, I picked myself up, dusted off my pants and got myself back on track. But they, our children, are on the trail; the split of the trail is right before their feet. I cannot run quick enough to catch them before they fall, the train is moving too fast. I cannot shout loud enough to warn them of this fatal danger ahead; the world is making too much noise and the television set is too loud. What am I supposed to do? Where do I begin? What am I supposed to say? How do I start? I may write such books, but who said I would be published broadly enough, let alone published at all? I may post informative status updates on my *Facebook* page and *Twitter*, but who said my people will listen? I may pour my heart out to my loved ones, but who said they will pay any attention? Up until this very day they haven't. Who said they will tomorrow? Who said I will be here tomorrow?

Satan, the delusionist, the deceiver, is not only among us but also within us. Because he has deceived us, we cannot recognize him, we even deny his very existence altogether. He has managed to disguise himself as a celebrity we watch in admiration on television, as a ruler we fight for in parliament, as a role model we look up to. But above all, he has managed to disguise himself as the God we call upon in worship through our religions. The Black child knows in his heart that God is All-Loving, and the Black child sees the images of this 'God' covered in white skin. The Black adult knows from experience that the white man has been sinful and devilish towards him and everyone else that looks like him. But now, how does the Black adult go about convincing the Black child that what he has been taught all along, is, in reality, false. How do I shift the misled mindset of the Black child from seeing God in the white man into seeing Him in everyone else including himself? Denying the god in him has created self-hatred and self-denial. He is ashamed of who and what he is, he is fearful of his future, embarrassed of his past, and ignorant of his present. Our communities are broken, and the only way to fix them is by fixing ourselves. Black intellectuals don't want to work together, they fear ideological clashes so they prefer working separately, and this is a major setback to Black progress. We can only truly rise as a unit; individualistic success is an illusionary success. In fact, it causes further division. The most important question in adults' minds today should be how do we go about re-instilling childhood into our children's lives? But the adult cannot think of such a question because he himself lacks adulthood – just as Blacks lack Blackness and human beings lack humanity. We dehumanize children by expecting them and pressurizing them to grow up and 'be' or 'become', as though childhood is humanless. Today I meet more humans than human beings. Amongst the minority who are human beings, I see more children than adults. Children are carefree, loving, forgiving, forgetful, compassionate, all-in-all. Children are *being human*, therefore are Human Beings. As they are the future, he who misleads children corrupts the future and defaces the beauty of a nation. Black kids have been the target of both biological and psychological genocide for hundreds of years under white cultural aggression. I call it "white cultural aggression" because it is the white man's natural culture to be hateful and aggressive towards Black people, anywhere he finds them. The inferiority-complex that we grew up suffering from as little kids is not inborn, it was systematically engineered through school education brain-washing processes and through media programming techniques that we call entertainment, from cartoon networks to talk shows. *H. Rap Brown* once said, *"Whatever you do not control can be used against you"*, and the Black man is still not the one in control of Black education and Black media, which is why our children continue to suffer and our next generation will also inherit the pain and suffering if we do not stand up and turn the tables around. This is a call, also, to Indians and Coloureds for they have rejected the Black reality of themselves and embraced the illusion of the semi-white character. According to *Basil Manning* of CARAS (Centre for Anti-Racism and Anti-Sexism), talking to *True Love Magazine* in an article titled *A Whiter Shade of Black:*

"In 1975, this country's education department

spent R1000 per annum on white kids, R340 on Indian children, R300 on Coloured children and R30 on each Black child". He adds, "That is how it caused Black kids to be ashamed of who they were, so many changed their names and tried to change the colour of their skins and hide their culture", says *Manning* and confessing, "The roots of me accepting the colour of my skin were in the 1970s and 80s, when I became aware of *Steve Biko* and the whole Black Consciousness movement. Before then, I wanted to be white and I saw my blackness as a problem. I saw people who were darker than I was as lesser, and myself as better because I was lighter. Once I became conscious, I stopped calling myself 'coloured' and called myself 'black born of mixed decent'.

Being Black, in this racist world; yes, it is a disadvantage, but no, it is not a disability. We can do and become whatever we want to. Black kids must be fed the truth as young as possible, as ugly and bitter as it is. We cannot raise them on lies anymore, as we were. Crippled as they may be from their childhood, children have to march forth, whether in a limp or even crawling on their stomach. Our children have to march forth.

May God make us good parents, may He grant us the will and enthusiasm to fulfill our duties as parents. May He grant us pious children who will happily fulfill their duties, which they owe to us as their parents and those they owe to You and to themselves.

CHAPTER 2

My Teenage Brother

A nation's youth is that nations' naked Truth

As a child, you listen to no one else but your parents, as a teenager – your friends, as an adult – yourself. As kids, bred by parents who lacked radical racial consciousness, we normally grow up with the same unfortunate fate. We went to school and met other ill-bred kids like ourselves. We came back home and played with other ill-bred kids in the neighborhood; we hung out with ill-bred siblings and cousins. Not surprisingly, we came into teenagehood and made friends with the same kind of kids, or same kids, who were now teenagers like ourselves.

As an unconscious teenager, what am I to learn from another unconscious teenager? What am I to teach him? Can we influence each other in any positive form? What have school teachers taught us about ourselves? What are the police doing to protect us, or are we the target?

Let's take a short journey back to my teenagehood. I remember my teenage self convinced that each of us are defined by the condition of the homes we come from: if you come from a rich family, I was convinced that you are better than those of us coming from less fortunate families. Maybe this was because the teachers treated you differently and your lunchbox was bigger.

I remember believing that kids that went to multi-racial schools were smarter than those who went to schools in the neighborhood. And those that went to predominantly white schools were even smarter. I remember idolizing the white race for I believed they were the only great intellectuals, inventors and philosophers, but I later lost interest in my *History* class because I could not relate to any of their heroes. I remember my heroes being 'street guys' who spoke slang and smoked weed and hung out on the street corners all day and night. I remember hating police so much because they used to circle my neighborhood in their huge drop-top 'hippo' trucks with rifles in their hands and hate in their faces. They hunted down and shot dead every street Brother with a brain. Now I understand they were sent to destroy potential, and they succeeded, but not for too long 'cos we are here now, and we will lead the revolution and we will breed more of our kind so that if they get us as well, the ship will not be left to sink, the movement will not be left alone to die. In Sunday School I remember the fun I had with friends and cousins and fellow worshipers playing sketches and singing in the choir. I remember Bible stories appearing to me like cartoons. I remember perceiving this pale and blue-eyed, long-haired, perfect-built, Caucasian Jesus as a heroic cartoon character. Even though I claimed to believe in him, I never really did. To me, even as a child, he was too unreal. He still is.

I remember the young girls I had crush on. I loved them deeply, so intensely and very dearly. Each crush was filled with fairytales and thoughts accompanied by heavy breaths and banging heartbeats. I had visions of them as my lifetime companions. Back then, love had no conditions – but that was an age of fantasy. I remember going to school being a drag, being unpleasant. Attending an Indian school, I remember Indian kids treated with care and consideration and Black students without. I remember the majority of Indian kids being better swimmers and better artists and students. And I remember that there was always that one Black student who was a better swimmer than all of them, a better artist than the rest and a better student in the entire school. I remember vividly my older Sister *Thabisile Hlatshwayo* was that student. On a broader scale, on the world scale, in music we have thousands of non-Black superstars, then we have *Michael Jackson*, Black and better than the rest; in Golf, *Tiger Woods*; Boxing, *Muhammad Ali*; Soccer, *Pele*; we have *Michael Jordan* in Basketball, while having countless intellectuals. And now I understand that a skillful artist is made, but a gifted one is born. I remember understanding absolutely nothing that was being taught in school and started bunking my classes. But now I understand why; I was being taught to become one of *them*, to become white - for they too (the Indians), had been whitewashed and I was made to reject who I am, to become ashamed and embarrassed for being Black. The word 'Black' was only mentioned in Slavery *Chapters*, in which whites were still glorified, even as ruthless invaders, rapists, murderers and colonists. No school subject taught me about who I was and where I came from. We were never taught anything about the condition of a Black man. No one taught me about our Black heroes; strictly Black heroes for Black people, not Black heroes for white people. No one said anything about *Steve Biko*. Why isn't his book *I Write What I Like* included in our curriculum? At least only in the Black schools. White kids might not *want* to hear anything about a man like him, but Black kids *need* to. But that will never be so, because it will awaken the Black youth and when the youth awakens, something happens, something moves, something changes – and it is that change that they do not want to see. No one taught me anything about *Robert Sobukwe*. Even though learners may learn about him in History classes today, but who decides what and what not to be taught? Isn't it the white man? It is. They run everything in this country. You are not told what you are *not supposed* to know. The way things are run is called *the System* for a reason, nothing occurs randomly, everything is systemized, planned out articulately. In the book *The Miseducation of The Negro, Dr Carter G. Woodson*, wrote, *"Blacks are the only group of people who take their most precious possessions, their children, and ask their oppressors to educate them and to mold and shape their minds."*

Firstly, we teach our youth how to live – and how to make a

living, then how to make money and how to maintain it. South Afrikan youth have this basic lesson to learn: in school you are taught how to work, while life teaches you how to live. Therefore, tertiary education is of secondary importance and life lessons are of primary importance, and the former will definitely destroy your character if you are not well educated on the latter. Fortunately, life lessons have no closing registration dates; however, they do have tuition fees – *sacrifice for knowledge!* If you don't understand what is happening within you, you will not see what is happening around you. You are probably shaking your head calling me foolish, because what you see you believe is all there is to see – you see a Black Minister in *Education* and a Black Minister in *Correctional Services*, even more so, a Black President. Therefore, you think I am crazy by blaming the so-called white man for he has long gone; but I say he is not gone, not now, not ever. This will be revealed in the following chapters. For now, quoting one of the greatest Islamic scholars, *Imam Shaikh Imran Housein* on white colonist rule, he said:

> "When they colonize a part of the world, they do not leave, they do not de-colonize, until and unless they have put in place institutions which will ensure that that society will continue to be ruled by them, by proxy. And in the process they seek to transform the rest of mankind into carbon copies of themselves."

This is definitely not to say that Black ministers are

blameless, we will come to them shortly. However, the struggling Black man needs to understand how the white man first colonized you, and then as from 1994, how he neo-colonized you. You are not free, not yet. You have been lied to and now you are perpetually lying to yourself.

An African delegate to the Third International Anglican Liturgical Consultation in York in 1989 defined colonialism as "Europeans telling Africans how to be Europeans while neo-colonialism is Europeans telling Africans how to be Africans." – passage extracted from *The Prophetic Witness in South Africa.*

South Afrikan Blacks we are so misinformed that when you start talking about Pan-Afrikanism and Pan-Afrikanist leaders such as *Sobukwe* and *Biko* (whose portraits you will never find hanging in corporate offices of so-called BEEs) we are the ones to object first and call you racist. The *Madiba Syndrome* has lulled our fighting genes back to sleep, back into unconsciousness. We have been romanced with oxymoronic words such as *'Peace In Our Land', 'Rainbow Nation', 'New South Africa'*, and national holidays such as *'Freedom Day', 'Day of Reconciliation', 'Humans Rights Day'*, amongst others. All the Black people 'up there' are nothing but faces with no voices. The decision maker is still the white elite behind the scenes, who make sure that the wealth of this country remains in white hands, who are the minority of this land, let alone settlers. If we are now truly living in the new South Afrika, what is new about it? Let us evaluate: who had better education system and better schools during apartheid? Whites! Who does today? Whites! Who had better jobs and better living? Whites! Who does this day? Again, Whites! Therefore, it is an insult to the intelligence of the People to tell them about what you call 'new' and then not be able to point out any change, any improvement.

As teenagers we grow up seeing such things though we can't solve or handle them, which causes us anger and frustration, and we feel neglected or perhaps betrayed by those who don't understand our frustrations. We carry these feeling with us as we approach adulthood. We spend most of our time trying to locate the source of all this anger. Those among us who find the answer to these questions first become revolutionaries, intellectuals, and leaders; but these new leaders fight for the People genuinely until they are offered high positions, which obviously is accompanied by fortune and fame, and then all of a sudden they no longer represent the People to the Government, but rather represent the Government to the People. Tragically, the rest, which is the majority, is still yet to learn, if only they live long enough and had a stronger will.

May God strengthen our will to learn, and may He teach us all that we need to know, and may He soften our hearts and sharpen our minds.

CHAPTER 3

My hustler brother

We learnt from hustlers that being notorious can make you big (pun intended)

Although high school was an unpleasant experience, most of us managed to graduate, some of us dropped out. Others among us failed their Matric and never went back to school again. During an unpleasant teenagehood in the township, filled with character flaws and self-identity crisis, some of us resorted to crime, some of us did drugs, drank alcohol, committed suicide, drowned ourselves in fashion trends (which is also a sickness), excessive promiscuity, party life and/or resorted to solitude. Those who opted for solitude were highly likely to suffer Depression, which is another gateway to suicide, alcohol, drugs, excessive sex, etc. Solitude can also lead to self-awareness, enlightenment, self-determination, and self-knowledge.

I remember my high school years; I mingled with Brothers from different townships. Every other day they would trade stories about hustlers in their neighborhoods – who did what, where and how. Car thieves and jackers, sharp shooters and criminals as they are, traditionally, the 'talk of the town' in Black communities. I remember them being heroic figures in our eyes. They had everything a ghetto teenage boy would fantasize about; fame, pretty girls, money, fancy cars, expensive clothes, expensive jewelry, and respect – in summary, they had *power*. We were young and ignorant, so were they. There was no other way we knew how to get all this at once. I do not remember any lawyer with fancy jewelry and plenty of women. Back then, I did not know any doctor with fame and a celebrity lifestyle. I do not remember any schoolteacher with fortunes. Can you blame us? One knew very well that one can be a successful hustler overnight and obtaining a Degree takes years of struggle and it's not even guaranteed. Every youthful soul wants to be seen, noticed, and talked about – admired in some way. We know that a white boy can get almost any Indian, Coloured, or Black girl he wants, simply because he is white, for our beautiful women have been firmly conditioned into believing that being white is the highest social and racial status. We know that a Coloured guy can scoop up almost any of our beautiful Black Sisters simply by being Coloured: "he has an English surname, he's light-skinned, he can't speak Zulu" they brag to one another – that alone sets him apart, makes him 'better'. My Black Sister wants that English surname more than anything– *Zama Jackson, Andiswa Philips, Kuli Roberts,* etc. is how she imagines herself in the near future. But, we also know very well that we can't have any white girl we like, or Indian or Coloured, nor, to some extent, even our own kind – because we are Black. We have to work extra hard and have to have something tangible to show for it. When I look at myself, at my language, my accent, my complexion, my kinky hair, my Afrikan name and last name, I immediately know that I can't impress them; I'm too Black! Therefore, I have to have a name (fame), money, power, respect, and/or anything of material wealth, something I can show off with.

Education has slain us, those who strove through the slain couldn't afford to study any further after completing high school, those who could were few, and we are very proud of them because they are part of us and they represent us all – lest they forget! The quickest way we knew how to get admiration was and still is through criminalized activities; sports and art comes second, then comes education. We love education but the Educational System never loved us. However, this is not to say that we as hustlers are not educated, we are, and we are as brainwashed as our so-called educated Brothers are. The 'street-life' survival, the slang, lingo, was invented by Black street-intellectuals not some dumb-head criminals. It was invented and practiced by smart Black men who wanted to, and in fact did, prove the system wrong and exposed it for what it is. Today it is very clear to every non-conformist that 'education' does not give you an education. We know now that the so-called Justice System was not meant to protect it's citizens but to control them; the economic system to enslave them; the social system to lock us within the borders drawn by them. These Black intellectuals were then called names such as rebels, criminals, thugs, gangsters etc.

"Slang is popular speech, the everyday

language of real men and women; often, too, it's camouflage, a lexicon of dissimulation and secrecy, beyond the reach of jargon, which is created by intellectuals and specialists, by people with power and wealth". (It provokes the riles, is profane and rough and defies authority). - *Critical Lives*, Andy Merrifield.

Teenagers grow up angry, feeling betrayed by the government and the system, and they do whatever to defy it and get what they should have gotten by any means – you buy a college textbook; I buy a gun. You buy a car; I jack it. You make a name in your firm, I earn street cred. You get a raise; I get Money Power Respect! *You can't tell me nothing!* This is the angry ghetto boy's mentality. We leant from the hustlers that being notorious can make you big. Once my hustling Brothers learn where this 'hustling game' came from, who it came from, and why, once we learn that it was only meant to fight and survive under this unjust system that keeps us impoverished and enemies to one another, we will stop killing our own kind. We will defend our own by any means necessary. But today, the so-called hustler, the thug – who is he hustling? A Black man. Who is he thugging? A Black man. Our very own Brothers are a threat to the Black community, they are number one enemies to Black progress, they steal from their people, they kill them, they pull them down, even our biggest hustler Brother called The Government is doing everything in its power to keep us down and out. The thug, the hustler, the criminal, originally, is the defender, the guard, the caretaker of the neighborhood. In our eyes, he is a Son, a Brother, a Father, but in the eyes of the law, he is nothing but an outlawed criminal, who deserves being shot dead or locked away forever. His enemy is the unjust system, not his neighborhood. If he thugs his fellows, he is a snitch, and a snitch is a danger to the community. He has gone insane from drug abuse, paralyzed by prison time, and lost direction from false politics. Still, I charge him Innocent. Who is guilty, the one who uses drugs or the one who makes them? Who is guilty, the one being lied to or the lair? Therefore, I charge the drug distributors and the lairs and hypocrites in our government and their banker allies, not my hustler Brothers trying to make a living the only way they know how, the only way the system has taught them. Truth is, the Black mans' condition requires urgent attention, and this is not unfairness, it's retributive justice. The Black masses are still following far behind due to injustices of the past, it's been twenty-one years under Black leadership yet we are still waiting for reparations. We don't want equality, we want justice. 'Equality' is an illusion of justice; it can never produce social order.

The modern day hustler – this is the ignorant Brother, he is a lost soul; lost in misconceptions, deceptions, lies and propaganda. This Brother is feared by the white community, and loved by the white elite. He is loved by the white elite only because he is very useful to him, he is very lucrative. This is the Brother who snatches handbags, steals cars, does house breakings, robs banks, steals cell phones, etc. Normally, this is a Brother that didn't finish school, he smokes, drinks, disrespects women, is inconsiderate towards other Black Brothers, and generally *foolish*! There are so many relevant things that he does not know. He thinks that breaking into a white man's house will cause some harm to the white man and elevate him to some relevant level – the television set he stole, the sound system, the jewelry, the DVD player, the vehicle – rich white folks can buy those items from petty cash; on the other hand if you are caught inside their premises, you are shot dead, either by the racist home owner himself or racist police, or perhaps a foolish Black police thinking he is doing justice to mankind by murdering his own Brother instead of arresting him.

However, one could also rightfully shoot you dead simply by defending himself from your stupidity which could cause his death or injury. If you escape that you can go back to the township and sell those stolen goods cheap, drink your cash, smoke it, buy some white owned brand sneakers such as *Chuck Taylors* at an Indian owned *Ginger Bhagwandaz* store, and it is over. Obviously, you will go back for more and more and more. However, eventually you will be caught and locked away; now this is where you become useful to the white elite. These are the people who makes sure that you know nothing about the privatization of prisons, *'where white owned corporations lobby for laws that will enhance their profits while targeting, exploiting and suppressing the Black community.'* Your being in prison is money in their pockets; they need you in there and will stop at nothing to keep the money coming. While prisons are privatized, there are individuals and groups, Black and white, in the South Afrikan and world governments who also gain in this big business; who do you think owns all these tenders in prisons, from food supply, cleaning equipment supply, uniforms, construction? Just like these young kids who draw tattoos all over their bodies calling it being *free-spirited*; doing what they like but not knowing that the *'hippie'* culture was created and strategically designed by the CIA and US government, creating rebels with no cause for a greater cause, while the

Black-consciousness movements were creating rebels with a cause for a better cause. My hustler Brother also fell into this trap, not realizing that his lifestyle was designed for him and he is only a puppet on a string. In the book, which is one of my favorites, *Comments on the Society of the Spectacle*, French revolutionary writer *Guy DeBord* wrote:

> "It is always a mistake to try to explain something by opposing Mafia and the state: they are never rivals." He concludes, "The Mafia is not an outsider in this world; it is perfectly at home." *Guy DeBord* warns us that "The only aim is to hide, or at least to disguise as far as possible, the working of various *agreements which decide everything*", and went on to say: "Our society is built on secrecy, from the 'front' organizations which draw an impenetrable screen over the concentrated wealth of their members, to the 'official secrets' which allow the state a vast field of operation free from any legal constraint; from the often frightening secrets of *shoddy production* hidden by advertising, to the projections of an extrapolated future in which domination alone

writes off the likely progress of things whose existence it denies, calculating the responses it will mysteriously make."

If the white folk don't respect you, at least make sure they fear you, not because you got a gun in your hand but because you got a brain in your head. As my Brother *Mumia Abu Jamal* puts it, these *unconscious* Brothers *"do not know about Black History; resistance and rebellion, and they do not want to know, their eyes seek only the streets, that is their battleground, and the targets are each other."*

To your loving family you are a shame. To your caring community at large you are an embarrassment. Nevertheless, to the white supremacist elite, the enemy of lightness, you are loved, because of your role as a very lucrative commodity. The enemy is the only one that is happy about you being a criminal, he does not give a tiny damn whether you die or live, and why should he, when he knows there are millions like you out there. Look at the twelve and thirteen year olds in your township: they smoke drugs, they curse, uninformed, rude, ballistic, and chaotic – *televisionary trained*, of course not all of them, thank God for that. In the ghetto, we have two types of Brothers; *Revolutionaries* and *Televisionaries* – which one are you? Revolutionaries are the ones who are hungry and desperate for change, and you can see the difference in the lifestyle they live. They stand out from the rest but understand that they are part and parcel of the whole. Televisionaries are all over the place, they are loud even in their laughter, they are the ones running the show, so they think. They think life is all about dancing to *Big Nuz*, drinking alcohol, smoking weed, drawing tattoos and sleeping around while the enemy is making sure that our schools are unorganized and dull so that you would drop out and go out in the streets to *make him some money*; the same money that pays his child's tuition fees in some posh private school or university overseas. If you stick it out and stay in school and you are gullible enough, you get fed all the misinformation, the propaganda filled in textbooks and misled so that you will never know what is really going on and remain ignorant to clear facts and refuse the truth when you hear it, like you are doing right now.

"Beyond the despised rainbow nation, most whites in South Africa still harbor stereotype of the indigenous blacks as savages, immoral, rapists, thieves and unrefined. They still see black South Africans as slaves to sex, alcohol and drugs. They still see them as lazy, beasts and corrupt and impossible to civilize through education." – Extract from *Nigerian Muse* article: *Mandela and Mbeki; Whiteman's Lapdogs?*

In the eyes of the European settlers, so-called white South Afrikans, *Nelson Mandela* is the *only* decent Black man in this country, and the media makes sure it stays that way. But remember, my dear Brother, we love you, and we understand that you didn't choose this yourself – this life was chosen for you, you were set up, your skin colour and your supreme understanding and knowledge made you a target and an object of terrorism. You have been terrorized since the day you were born, even before, then they gave you a false description to the word *'terrorism'* to make you believe you are the one who is a terrorist. The Glorious Koran warned us that *"he (Satan) will threaten you with poverty and he will command you with immorality"*. But remember, Brother of mine, you can bear the pain of hunger, but you cannot bear the pain of *'hell fire'* – the guilt and shame. We understand that you have fallen for this trap; you have seen misery, you have tasted hunger and smelled death, and you are scared; be afraid not, Knowledge of Self and Unity is key to our victory, the good thing is that you are still here; you still have a chance to change and recreate your fate, God willing. One easy way of getting back to the enemy is through resistance; resist *his* stray lifestyle, *his* drugs, *his* alcohol, resist *his* prison, *his* education, resist bad company, go back to your natural self – reclaim your royalty. Read the *Glorious Koran*, read the *Holy Bible*, read the so-called *Book of the Dead*, read the *Torah*, this is your history, your story, your glory. Study Black history and Black books written by/about Black writers such as *Ngugi wa Thiong'o, Steve Biko, Chinua Achebe, Thabo Mbeki, Mumia Abu Jamal, Dr Khalid Al-Mansoor, bell hooks, Toni Morrison, George Jackson, W. E. B Du Bois, Frantz Fanon, Heuy P. Newton, Angela Davis, Malcolm X, Louis Farrakhan, Sojourner Truth, ZK Matthews.* Then you will realize that you were born beautiful, you were not born criminal, thug, hustler, or gangster. These are the names you were labeled with so you'd be confused and lost in ignorance about your true self, your true nature, but instead resemble these ugly name tags so that you will not only forget that you are a beautiful Black man but also see *Beauty* as a weakness. Therefore, you should be reminded my Beautiful Brother, that *Beauty* is a manifestation of *Strength, Love, Compassion, Freedom, Mercy, and Wisdom*, and you are exactly that, and that is exactly you. I love you with my soul and my love for you is solely for the sake of your liberation!

May God the Almighty strengthen our love for each other as Black Brothers, no matter which tribe one is born of, no matter the status, location or tongue.

CHAPTER 4

My White-Collar Brother

This is a new breed, a super human

This is a Black man who has a *profession*, therefore, is called a *professional*. For a very long time, wrongly, in the 'Black perspective', being a professional was only being either a lawyer, doctor, C.A, or C.E.O. And I remember, as a young kid, not seeing many Black professionals. I also remember that when seeing one, it would seem strange, like seeing a creature from a different planet. I remember having a desire to become like them – they were looked up to, talked about, stared at in amazement. As a little boy, seeing a Black man who was not struggling financially was not an everyday thing. We only saw these sort of Blacks in *Bona* and *Drum* magazines, and they were actors, singers, and sports personalities with huge homes. But seeing a financially stable ordinary Black person was very rare – it was a thing to watch and stare at.

I remember seeing these Brothers in big cars, Mercedes Benzes and BMWs, usually they wore prescription glasses, were well spoken, formally dressed, well groomed, and usually married with a very light-skinned beautiful Black Sister, as though she was compensating his desire for a white woman. There was nothing not to admire about this Brother, at least I saw absolutely nothing. Even though most of them still lived in the townships, still they seemed different from other Black Brothers. These Brothers, unlike most, finished high school and went to college/university, graduated with good grades. This was never a strange thing in a Black community at large, it still is not. But, in the area within the community that I come from, where I was born and raised, this was very rare, therefore, I wasn't used to it. Most Brothers in my neighborhood were in and out of prison, they would hang out in the street day and night, others pick pocketing, gambling, others just getting high, while others drunk their lives away. I remember thinking that these professional Brothers got where they were because they were smarter than the next Brother on the block. I would look at the struggling grown up Brothers in my neighborhood and think that if only they were smart as well they would have became doctors and lawyers and teachers, but because they were not, this is why they aren't even working. Only at a later age did I realize how wrong I was. Nevertheless, I am grateful that eventually I had this realization; most have not, especially our beloved professional Brothers themselves. Black South Afrikans have been impoverished for so long that it eventually became natural to associate poverty with Blackness and whiteness with wealth. It is not the other way around, hence, we associate *poverty with Blackness* not *Blackness with poverty*; *whiteness with wealth*, not *wealth with whiteness*. When one says "poor people" one automatically thinks of Black people, and this is a much more engraved kind of self-esteemlessness. It is so intense to the degree that when a Black man among us makes it rich we reject him and say things like "he is trying to be white", we say "he thinks he is better than us" – us the *Black* not us the *poor*, for we have long accepted poverty as part of being Black. On the other hand, those among us who become rich, they continuously use whiteness as the target point. And this is the sole reason in the process they themselves become whitened. They rush to the white neighborhoods, they want to drink what the white man drinks, eat what he eats, adopts the so-called white manner even to the very basics such as 'table manners', they wear what he wears and how he wears it. He measures all of his financial and social status by white standards, along the way losing his sense of self. It is great to lose your sense of Blackness for a sense of universality, but it is terrible to lose your sense of Blackness for whiteness. Being universal is God-like, it is a sense of viewing others as beings not according to their race, and that is how you view yourself as well. With this sense of realization, all of Man will unite. However, I strongly discourage my People to continue preaching this "*One Human Family*" message, we've been the only race preaching it and for so long, these are the kind of messages that are keeping us stagnant while every other race is moving up; we should preach "*Race First*" or no preaching at all!

Growing up into teenage hood, to my disappointment, I learnt that while my professional Brothers are 'kings' in our eyes, they are slaves in the white world. The Black lawyer we look up to in admiration is but a sub-servant in the white owned law firm. The chartered accountant we praise is but a subordinate to white superiors, and even worse, their white counterparts. For them, being around other Blacks gives them comfort – all the admiration and attention they receive from other Black people remediates their bruised egos and sooths the racial exploitation and discrimination they experience every day of their work lives, and when they work for, with, and within their own Black communities not in order to be looked upon but rather to uplift their own people, they will succeed in becoming real role models, instead of being professional slaves for white folks, working a job instead of building independent Black businesses. A job, any job, should not be mistaken for economic success or victory, because it is not. As *Dr Claude Anderson* explained the matter of the Black Brother in America, saying:

> "Only 2% of all the black folks in America work for their community, for their own people producing comfort and products for their own people. You have NOT moved one iota in 140 years in terms of employment. Our people still do not understand that you can NOT enrich yourself working a job. A job is NOT designed to enrich you. A job is designed to maintain you ... to keep you one week away from welfare, unemployment, and the food

stamp lines. If you want to get rich, you MUST move into a business and business ownership. Business will transfer and redistribute wealth 6 to 8 times faster than working a job. The only way you are going to get rich working a job is if you steal…."

They enjoy being spotted with their white colleagues. We see them sharing jokes and laughter. They paint a picture of a perfect multi-racial work relationship with love, fairness, colorlessness, and equality. And us, the Black observers, buy into it, while they know it's a big lie. It is all an act. Only to come to terms at an old age that life is not a movie. So, what was all the acting for, they ask themselves, so do we. It is not their fault, we reason, it is what being Black in a country ruled by white racists (even by proxy) have taught them, have taught all of us. They have been taught, like the rest of us, Indians and Colored as well, that being white is the ultimate goal. It is *the* thing to be, and it can be reached – by *anyone*. You just need to do these few little things (subconsciously) and you are sorted:

Replace the term Black for the term 'filth'.

Replace the term white for the term 'pure'.

Generate as much money as you possibly can, *by any means necessary*.

Be less religiously strict (even with your kids) and more secular, call it being 'open-minded', 'modern' or 'civilized'.

Strip off your Afrikanness and Westernize yourself. Look up to America and Europe as your model aspiration.

Dress like a French, drive like a German, eat like an Italian, and speak like an American.

To top it off, become an occasional Christian. This means that you are now only a Christian on Sundays (if you remember).

This is a new breed, a super human, who, all at once, can be both 'spiritual' and materially extreme, smart and superficial. This Brother has important things he overlooks and people he undermines, and vain things he upholds and cherishes. He is fond of his status; he smiles upon being called *Dr. Masuku* or *Adv. Mhlongo*. He loves being called 'Sir' more than being called *'Brother'*. 'Brother' translates to equality while 'Sir' can be understood as superiority. When being called *Sir., Dr., Prof., Adv., or Mr.*, he feels superior; therefore, he acts and talks likewise. In contrary, for a conscious Brother, being called *Brother* is the most honorable of all titles – it means we are equal, we are family, and we are *aware* of it. But how can a *Dr.*, a man of prestige, allow himself to be aligned with me, a high school drop-out who never had one decent job. How can an *Adv.* accept equality with a Brother who has been in and out of jail all his life. Yes, we might claim friendships due to our common goals, backgrounds, aspirations, salaries, and culture, but when it comes to family we have been deprived the freedom of choice. You cannot choose your family. I did not choose to be Black – did you? So whether we like it or not, and whether we accept it or deny it, we are Brothers and *nothing* divides us; not culture, not creed, title, salaries, qualifications, backgrounds, aspirations, taste in fashion, religion, location, mentality, or language. The bottom line is very simple: if you are Black, you are my Brother, and because I am Black, I am your Brother. My son is your son, your mother is my mother – our fathers are Brothers, therefore, we are family! May the Almighty God guide us.

CHAPTER 5

My Integrated brother

He's both tender-hearted and tender-minded

This is the most dangerous Brother of us all. This is also the most progressive Brother of us all; progressive in terms of multi-culturization. This Brother is capable of bringing all races and creeds together. When he is dangerous, he possesses the most threat to the de-culturalization and the unity of our (Black) community.

As a young boy, I had always seen white people as a

powerful race, superior and supreme, tall and well-built, intelligent and witty. That is how I was taught to see them. But I have also always had feelings of contempt towards them. I never really liked them, not because I was an evil child but because I was a righteous child who could spot evil in whatever form it assumes. Behind this contempt was a hidden knowledge. I knew very well that behind every evil act lies great fear, and in that fear lies great weakness. Since then I've always wanted to prove, at least to myself, how weak the white racist is, and I succeeded, like most Black intellectuals and revolutionaries of the past and present.

I remember experiencing great confusion accompanied by great agony whenever seeing a Black person, whether he be a gardener, security guard, servant, nanny, chauffer, waiter, or whatever his sub-servant job may be. I never liked seeing that, I still don't. My anger was born of desperation; it was my personal passive resistance struggle. I wanted to help these people. I wanted them to become lawyers and judges and business owners. I wanted to free them, both physically and psychologically. At first, I did not realize that there was something wrong, unnatural about this picture. I thought this is how things are meant to be, until I came into the realization that the social system we are living under is born of the government system, which is the 'umbrella' to all other smaller systems; social system, economic system, religious system, geographical system, etc. Having realized this, and learning that the white government and the white people (who obviously were in support of this colonial system, one way or another) are the cause of all our problems and suffering. Back then, seeing a Black person laughing with, dating, or befriending any white person, in my eyes was a sell-out. Why is he laughing with the enemy? How could he date a white woman? Is he blind to Black beauty? Who does he think he is? What are they talking about when drinking tea? How does she look this white man in the eye when making love? What does she see? I would ask myself. Troubled!

Back then, we did not know much, we were kids. We did not experience a lot of violence, and personally, in '94 I was doing Grade 7. In 1990, which was the 'release' year of *Mandela*, I was in Grade 3. So, by then, everyone was happy and positive, no one was angry anymore. Black folks were told to be peaceful and join hands with whites – but on the other hand, the white man was behind the greatest bloodbath between the IFP, UDF and the ANC, which left thousands of our poor Brothers dead. Unfortunately, thousands more of our IFP and ANC, and even more so COPE, EFF and NFP, Black Brothers are still going to kill each other in the near future if they don't wake up from the slumber of ignorance, where again, the white man will be the puppeteer. Today, in 2015, 21 years after 'liberation', nothing has changed. Yet, it is made to look as though everything has. Black people are still oppressed in different aspects, still feeling a great sense of self-inferiority, subservient, lost, desperate and hungry. In an article by *Nigerian Muse*, where Mandela is labeled a *'modern day martyr blinded by amnesia'*, the writer states

"Within his universe and as a man of dignity, Mandela has a grand, yet opaque vision of racial integration, even if forced. But the white South Africans are clever enough to extricate themselves from the emotional unreality of racial integration and the perceived reality of their superiority."

The sad, yet, funny thing is that the integrated Blacks living in the predominantly 'white neighborhoods' actually believe that it is 'their' neighborhood too. However, by the look of things, by how reality has always been since the European colonizers arrived and settled in this country, it is otherwise. They are overlooking a few key facts. They might live there, afford what the white man affords, eat what and where the white man eats, talk like him, befriend him, but the fact remains that they are a settler in the settlers' neighborhood. You are an unwelcome stranger, who constantly has to prove yourself both in terms of intelligence and wealth. In the 'white' neighborhood, the Black man constantly has to prove his compatibility, his prestige, his IQ (Intelligence Quotient), but most crucially, his innocence. He has to prove that he is well educated, that he has a profession, a career, a business, and not rich from criminal or athletic activities, or even political connections. Moreover, if he smiles more, laughs louder, and maintains more eye contact, he is given a chance to prove his pureness, his gentlemanlyness, his 'good' manners, in short; his whiteness. If he is approved, he can now officially establish himself up there with the Caucasians and eventually *almost* fit in – for he can never perfectly do so, because the upper-class suburb establishment is an *Apartheid establishment* that was designed by whites for "*WHITES ONLY*", and it is still under the rule and governance of its architects. In *The Wretched of the Earth*, French revolutionary writer *Frantz Fanon* observes both white and Black towns:

"(The settler's) feet are protected by strong shoes although the streets of his town are clean and even, with no holes or stones. The settler's town is a well-fed town, an easygoing town; its belly is always full of good things. The settler's town is a town of white people, of foreigners. The town belonging to the colonized people, or at least the native town, the Negro village, the medina, the reservation, is a place of ill fame, peopled by men of evil refute. They are born there, it matters little where or how; they die there, it matters not where nor how. It is a world without spaciousness; men live there on top of each other, and their huts are built one on top of the other. The native town is a hungry town, starved of bread, of meat, of shoes, of coal, of light. The native town is a crouching village, a town on its knees, a town wallowing in the mire. It is a town of niggers and dirty arabs. The look that the native turns on the settler's town is the look of lust, a look of envy; it expresses his dream of possession – all manner of possession: to sit at the settler's table, to sleep in the settler's bed, with his wife if possible. The colonized man is an envious man. And this the settler knows very well; when their glances meet he ascertains bitterly, always on the defensive 'They want to take our place'. It is true, for there is no native who does not dream at least once a day of setting himself up in the settler's place."

Although *Fanon* wrote this five decades ago, this is a 2015 real life experience for millions of Black South Afrikans. I would highly advise people of other racial backgrounds to visit at least two townships in their lifetime. I would highly advise my integrated Brother to speak about his township experience, if he has any. And I want all the people to understand that the township experience is not the *Black experience*, it is however, the harsh condition of the Black man as systematically designed by the evils of the white colonist rule.

I read in *Al-Qalam* some time ago, an Islamic newspaper, *January 2012* issue, an article called *Open Talk,* under the heading *KwaMashu: 'My little peak down the road'*, written by my Indian Muslim Sister named *Shubnum Khan* after a short township tour. She wrote:

> "Townships in South Africa are not a place you want to get lost in – especially *KwaMashu* which was recently honored with the title of South Africa's murder capital. Townships are

the sort of things that bogey man stories are made of in our society – we pass them, we never go in them and we fear what goes on there". She continues, "there were many issues I had with this trip. I didn't know what to feel about the group's white people who played with local children and spoke to adults about their problems. Was this part of the tour? Part of some act we're supposed to play on a township tour – sympathize with the locals?"

Different year and different era compared to Fanon but same issues. As we re-visit and re-analyze the condition of the Black man in the twenty-first century while re-teaching our 'born-frees' who may be lost in confusion as to what Apartheid really is. We shall teach them, for if we don't, our enemies will. Apartheid and Racism are not historical disasters that took place once upon a time in the pre-Democratic South Afrika. Apartheid is a systematically engineered operation meant to last forever despite who the President is. Many do not know that it was not the Afrikaner

(Boer) who designed this gruesome system. It was the British, the Englishman, Sir George Grey in particular, and the Boers were only responsible for implementing it thoroughly and whole-heartedly as they were instructed. The English always came with a smile and the Dutch, the Boer, with a growl, but the biting was the same. Then came a bloody battle between these two power-hungry beasts. Remember the Anglo-Boer War, the Englishman and the Boer killing one another over a land that belongs to neither of them, in a land where they were both no longer welcome guests? The land of your ancestors; the holy Motherland. This needs to be understood: when we address and write about Apartheid and Racism issues, we are not "stuck in the past" as many claim, we are rather fighting a colonial System that is still in full operation in spite of Black leadership, who have no interest or whatsoever in destroying it.

My integrated Brother is blind to all this – he is blind to the system. He is both tender-hearted and tender-minded. The sole reason for this premature integration is the belief born of inferiority complex, whether individually or collectively. It is the belief that with a white person 'you can go very far', 'you can reach higher heights', 'You can go further'; that you can do much better with one than you can without one. A Black woman marrying a white man, she is assured that she is set for life. She feels very secure therefore very confident and comfortable. A Black guy dating a white girl feels supreme and superior to his Black Brothers because they are dating Black women, like themselves. He believes he is a thousand steps ahead of them, his social status is marvelous – he cannot be compared with. How wrong he is! These integrated Blacks (especially young women), were they not the first ones (in great numbers) among their race to smoke cigarettes ... then in public? Were they not the first ones to smoke weed and cocaine and other drugs? To use swear words and derogatory terms? Today the situation is even more shameful and embarrassing – beautiful Black women throwing themselves upon white men, no matter how dumb, ugly, stupid, heartless and ruthless one is. Why are they so desperate? Why are we all so desperate? We call this liberation and freedom of choice – we say 'things are different now, it's unlike before – we are all the same and equal – what's the big deal ... what's all the fuss about....?' We say. But I say, men are not equal in the eyes of racial justice and economical freedom. Some men believe that other men should be kept in slavery, for slaves are cheap labor – we all like beautiful things, but how many are willing to pay the price for them? Therefore, we need slaves; we need the poor, we need outlaws, hooligans, the broke and desperate, we need beggars, because beggars cannot be choosers – and we need them for our own good, our personal and selfish gain, but we will call this 'job opportunities.' He who is not Black conscious does not have any idea whatsoever on what is going on in his own mind because he doesn't have Knowledge of Self. As *Frantz Fanon* wrote:

> "The Antillean [the Antilles is a French colonized island off the coast of Africa] has therefore to choose between his family and European society, in other words, the individual who climbs up into society – white and civilized – tends to reject his family – black and savage."

Without any form of criticism, but merely observation; nowadays you find Black Brothers who are caught up in this secular mentality and system dating white women or being friends with white kids. This very same system teaches them that white people are better beings, they are civilized and you are not. It teaches that being Black is a plague that you can only cure by 'whitening' yourself. It teaches them that Black people are physically strong, yet mentally weak (by nature), and white people are physically weak yet very smart, also, by nature, so, it is okay that we let them run things, run companies, design strategies, and point where 'a strong Black man' should stand, where he should walk, where and how he should pack those loads of boxes. Black folks today, young and old, delight in being seen with white peers, who have no fundamental connection whatsoever with them.

"One might wonder if this social connection is really necessary. If a young person has found a niche among a circle of White friends, is it not really necessary to establish a Black peer group as a reference point? Eventually it is. As one's awareness of the daily challenges of living in a racist society increases, it is immensely helpful to be able to share one's experiences with others who have lived it. Even when White friends are willing and able to listen and bare witness to one's struggles, they cannot really share the experience." – *Beverly Daniel Tatum*, from the book, *Why Are All The Black Kids Sitting Together In The Cafeteria.*

Integration is okay and it is a lovely and a wonderful thing to see. God and all His Prophets (peace and blessings be upon them) did not promote it but nevertheless they acknowledged it. And for a nation like ours, the Black nation, which is still re-developing in terms of Self-awareness and still has a long way to go, too much integration can cause us to stumble, it can cripple us in many ways. Too much integration had, and will continue to shut our eyes from recognizing racism and racially derogatory statements and gestures. There are no other Black people who experience racism nearly as much as integrated Blacks but they do not and cannot see it; they will, however, as soon as they step back just a little and spend some time with disintegrated indigenous-language-speaking Black people. Towards the end of his life, the most famous Black integrationist, *Dr Martin Luther King Jnr.*, wrote:

"I must confess that over the past few years I have been gravely disappointed with the white moderate. I have almost reached the regrettable conclusion that the Negro's great stumbling block in his stride towards freedom is not the White Citizen's Councilor or the Ku Klux Klanner, but the white moderate, who is more devoted to "order" than to justice; who prefers a negative peace which is the absence of tension to a positive peace which is the presence of justice; who constantly says: 'I agree with you in the goal you seek, but I cannot agree with your methods of direct action'; who paternalistically believes he can set the timetable for another man's freedom: who lives by a mythical concept of time and who constantly advises the Negro to wait for a

> 'more convenient season.' Shallow understanding from people of good will is more frustrating than absolute misunderstanding from people of ill will. Lukewarm acceptance is much more bewildering than outright rejection."

My Brothers and Sisters, this is what integration seeks; to indirectly pull all the strings in your way of thinking and to set up boundaries, not only politically or socially, but also in the various business endeavors. The so-called white moderate plants seeds in your mind and waters them and you are unaware of this, that when they have grown and producing fruits you take all the credit thinking it was all your idea, for example, the idea of *Black Feminism* which is the mastermind of the white male meant to destabilize the Black family structure and destroy the *Blackpower* revolution. In the same book referred to above, Black American author *Beverly Daniel Tatum* took serious offence to what almost all integrated 'independent' Black women would have smiled at and felt honored by. She wrote: *"Following a presentation I gave to some educators, a White man approached me and told me how much he liked my ideas and how articulate I was. "You know", he concluded, "if I had had my eyes closed, I wouldn't have known it was a Black woman speaking". (I replied, "This is what a Black woman sounds like").*

As *Dr Bobby Wright* warned us: *"The evil of racism prevails best when its victim no longer recognizes it."*

We, as Black people, have to remain aware without being prejudiced, therefore we have to remember that *Racism* is our enemy not *generally* white people as individuals, who are partaking in this extravaganza perhaps without a deep or any consciousness of the implications of it, both upon the Black race and also upon themselves. This is not to say that white people are unaware of all their racist tendencies, they fully and arrogantly are, and they must be thoroughly crushed each time they try it because white people test you and if you let it slide they do or say something worse the next time. If you do not know who your enemy is, you will not know what he is doing to you, and you might just find yourself helping him in destroying you. The arrogant white masses is the helper, the benefactor, and the weapon of this racist system. And if the word *Devil* is an attribute to the one who *De-values* – then in relation with other races, the collective White Race is, indeed, the Devil; as we have been witnessing his super *de-valuation* system called *Apartheid* and *White Supremacy* (which is in fact *White Racial Aggression*), that which has crushed long-standing prestigious dynasties and enslaved every race in the world. It has massacred and colonized nations, and ruthlessly slaughtered innocents – from men, women, to children, and there is no need to tell him what he has done to mankind, he knows very well. Despite all his bestiality, ask any Black man, integrated or not, and he will guarantee you that "white people are naturally civilized and good-mannered". But what exactly is civil about this man? *Somebody answer me!* This is because the white man made it clear to the world that by butchering all the worlds' native inhabitants and their dignified cultures, traditions and religions, and giving them a new god, he is doing them a favor; he is actually civilizing them and the entire human population. If this is the case, then we do not want his kind of civilization! Do not fall for it Black man, let him keep it to himself and his people. Legendary Black writer, Mama *Toni Morrison* said,

"Racism is a construct; a social construct. And it has benefits. Money can be made off of it. People who don't like themselves can feel better because of it. It can describe certain kinds of behavior that are wrong or misleading. So (racism) has a social function. But race can only be defined as a human being."

The white man, too, is in trouble, in trouble with his conscience (if he has any) which he deals with by adopting a Black child or feeding the so-called poor while doing absolutely nothing about eradicating his class beneficiary stronghold called *Racism* – which essentially is the cause of Black poverty in the first place. Therefore, he is guilty and will continue to pay the price and suffer the consequences for his bloody hands until he also joined the struggle in putting a stop to this evil he created. This is only a friendly warning to my beloved white brothers. May God soften their hearts and make them strong in His Divine Governance.

CHAPTER 6

My Christian Brother

The Black-on Black Conflict

Starting this Chapter, we ought to examine the Christian/Tradition relation conflict, with each being the main obstacle to growth of the other. Christianity is and has been an obstacle for the Black Tradition to grow both in sophistication and in dominance. On the other hand, the 'Black' Tradition has also played a major role causing stagnancies in the growth of Christianity.

Most Black Christians who also practice their 'Black' tradition and rituals would justify their actions by quoting the biblical verse where Jesus (pbuh) says that he did not come to change the ways and practices of the people but rather he came to strengthen them. The 'Traditional Christian' is failing to rationalize this statement, why? Because he is half Christian and half Traditionalist. Jesus (pbuh) was sent to remind the Jews about "The Law" and the commands of God, the Almighty, the Creator, as brought to them by Prophet Moses (pbuh). He was sent as another reminder because the people he was sent to, i.e. the Jews, had forgotten and went astray. But, what was this Command of God? This command is the very same Command that all the Prophets who came before him were sent to teach; the Command is: *God is One, he is Alone. No one is worthy of worship but God, Alone*. This Command is the fundamental doctrine of Judaism, Christianity, and Islam, and without this Command, the religion is corrupted, completely. Therefore, our beloved prophet Jesus (peace be upon him) was sent to his people, the Jews, to rectify any and every practice which seemed against this Command – and everything else that was deviating from the Commandments of God. For example, there were people who worshiped idols (gods, the dead, angels, statues such as golden calves, kings etc.). Obviously this practice is totally against Gods' Command. Therefore, Jesus (pbuh) was sent to rectify this practice. In South Afrika, in particular, the Black traditionalist would stand firm in affirmation that he does not worship the dead; he would say that he respects them and he remembers them but no he does not worship them. But who does he turn to for help? Does he not kneel down and invoke the names of his forefathers, asking them for good luck and blessings, and asking them for light and guidance? Does he not? He knows he does. Our pure Afrikan traditional religion is to invoke the name uMvelinqangi, the Creator of Heavens and Earth, the real Afrikan God who is not an ever angry God and threatening like the European God, rather the Merciful, the Sustainer. This is the God our ancestors told us about, this is the God they worshipped. From the book titled *Archbishop Tutu: Prophetic Witness in South Africa*, I quote; Bishop Tilewa Johnson who speaks of how Anglican converts in Gambia resisted missionary pressure to abandon indigenous thoughts and practices by holding on to them in secret. *"On top we behaved as Christians"*, he confesses, *"but deep down we had another God, a real African God, whom we turned to when we were in trouble"*.

Millions of my Christian Brothers have suffered and are still suffering this conflict. Traditionalists and Africanists of the past rejected the whole idea of the Church and Christianity for they strongly felt that this doctrine twists the true teachings of uMvelingqangi, hence they called it 'ukusonta', meaning 'to twist' or 'to bend'. The accusation was that "*basonta iNkolo yethu, iNkolo yesiNtu*" (they are twisting and corrupting our Afrikan belief system). Pro-black Africanists distanced themselves from Christianity as much as possible, and they, instead, felt much more comfortable and connected with the teachings of Islam, which has the highest number of followers in the Afrikan continent. Perhaps this is because Islam is in line with Afrikan cultural religion such as the practice of polygamy, and it does not forbid any nation, tribe, and family to *remember* their dead and also to slaughter in their remembrance and all blessed things done in the Name of uMvelingqangi/God. These are two of the most upheld traditional practices – polygamy and ancestry. In the very same book; *Prophetic Witness in South Africa, St. Irenaus* says: *"The glory of God is the living human person, which here means believers fully alive, enabled to praise God with their cultural values"*. This is also how the Africanists felt. They did not want to be turned into something they are not and told to believe in what they do not understand. No real human being would want that for himself, as *Archbishop Tutu* said:

> "With part of himself (the African Christian) has been compelled to pay lip service to Christianity as understood, expressed and preached by the white man. But with an even greater part of himself, a part he has been often ashamed to acknowledge openly and which he had struggled to repress, he had felt that his Africanness was being violated. The white man's largely cerebral religion was hardly touching the depths of his African soul, he was being redeemed from sins he did not believe he had committed; he was being given answers to questions he had not asked".

This is the Black-on-Black conflict that the Black South Afrikan Christian Brother has been and still is dealing with, consciously or sub-consciously. This dual-characteristic is a clear indication that something needs to be corrected, and urgently, not by the Roman Catholic or the Anglican, rather by us as Black men in Christianity. May God give us patience, wisdom, and understanding.

The New Age Christian Brother

Christianity has developed a new age culture, which also has, unsurprisingly, created a new kind of Christian Brothers and Christian Sisters. This is a post '94, 'New South Afrika' creation – filled with Freedom, in every sense of the word. In this time and age, this is the most influential Brother of them all – and this is a great compliment. This Brother is clean-shaven, immaculately dressed, usually in tailored business suits, well-groomed, with the look that is regarded 'acceptable'. This Brother is the master of the 'welcoming' appearance, with the look that subconsciously declares: *"I'm not one of them, those typical Blacks who rob and steal"*, you know those who speak slang, sag their pants with *All-Stars* and caps? Despite all the effort, he later learns that this is how all Black men are judged.

I choose Christianity as my point of focus for the same reason I will choose the ANC on the following Chapter, *My Political Brother*. The reason is that in this country, Azania (South Afrika), at this point in time, these are the two dominant groups, not only in the Black communities but also nationwide. And in matters of politics and religion it is the dominant groups that have the most influence on the general social behavior of the citizens.

I remember as a child going to church. I would see all these well-mannered, well-dressed, well-spoken young and grown respectable Black men. They moved about the church gently, shaking hands and exchanging kind words – *"in the name of Jesus"* being their motto. The ladies would dress formal as well, yet stylish and trendy and some elegant. Single Brothers keeping their eyes open for potential partners, and girls and women would also peep for potential husbands; most preferably the one whose family is well known in the church, most talked about. The most ideal was the one who is most religious, liked by the leading priest, has a car and a very good job, trendy with a good qualification under his belt. In those times, our pastors were modest and kind, and quite serious about their reputation. Nowadays I notice that pastors and preachers are obliged to become some sort of entertainer; they *have* to be funny and lively in order to keep the people awake otherwise people are going to get bored and sleep, which will likely lead to them leaving the church and joining another more energetic and entertaining one. They are socially and religiously 'liberal' on child raising, and don't they allow our women and children to wear skinny pants, tight and short skirts, even to church? Don't we mingle freely with members of the opposite sex, inside and outside of church? Before we go any further, this must be mentioned – again, we base all these essays on generalization. Therefore, we are referring on the mentality of the majority within the group – this has nothing to do with a pious, God-fearing Christian Brother and Sister.

Spreading the Word of God is beautiful but dividing ourselves causes us to judge. Where I come from, my Christian Brothers open new churches every other day. Once he achieves some sort of celebrity status, he starts his own church and brings his wife along, just like in a family business venture. His wife becomes his co-regent, teaching men and preaching to them, and men sit quietly, in contradiction to a Biblical message: *"Women should listen and learn quietly and submissively. I do not let women teach men or have authority over them. Let them listen quietly. For God made Adam first, and afterward he made Eve. And it was the woman, not Adam, who was deceived by Satan, and sin was the result." – 1 Timothy, 2:11.*

As a thoroughly Westernized religion, Christianity has lot to answer for, especially regarding the condition of the Black man in this country. To become what it is today, Christianity had to be secularized by the European elite, the Roman Empire and the current Western imperialists, all to fulfill their godless political/economical goal. In it's so-called evolution, Christianity has taken a secular route and adopted the idea of *'come as you are, no matter what you are wearing or what your lifestyle is, God wants your heart not your clothes or personality'*. Perhaps this was a strategy used to increase the number of followers of the faith, but it's hard not to think it was also an attempt to de-culturize every indigenous culture, or simply an attempt to westernize all indigenous cultures while de-Christianazing Christendom under the banner of 'Evolution'. They called this 'modernization' but, in reality, one doesn't have to be Western to be modern. And since Black people of this country, after Nigerians, are the most culturally westernized or 'modernized' compared to other Blacks in the continent, and has a majority of Christians, in recent years we have seen a number of mainstream Christian followers emigrating from and rejecting their 'rigid' churches for the newly invented liberal ones. We have seen an even greater number of non-church goers, non-religious, non-God-fearing people also going to these newly invented churches full of worldly freedom and godless liberation. Since then we have heard many stories that are devious about the church experience. We saw more things that are devious inside the church than ever before. Skirts went up and then upper, dresses became tight and then tighter, heels became high and higher, hair became greasy and greasier, nails long and longer, lips glossy and glossier, voices loud and louder, more laughter, more gossip, love became less, and pockets became full while hearts became empty; immorality at its best. Even more confusing is the relationship between church members and political parties, and church leaders and politicians, where most of them are proudly and openly members or supporters of the ANC, DA, COPE, SACP, NFP, IFP, etc. etc., and telling their followers what to vote for during local and national elections, when, instead, they should be focusing on revolutionalizing this country into a Christian state. I would personally love that because guaranteed our youth will follow suit, for they always resemble the system of the state, but instead, my Christian Brother gives all his energy and support to this godless secular system which stands for everything the Bible is against; same-sex marriages, prostitution, abortion, unjust laws, and public sale of alcohol and firearms. It would not shock me to learn that these new churches are formed or funded by different political organizations for a political agenda and their Pastors are, in reality, political agents preaching *Capitalism*, disguised as preachers of the Gospel, or perhaps they are preachers who have been bought and became political agents. This is indeed confusing because naturally people join political parties seeking the solution to social, economical, racial, or political injustices and problems that they may be facing at the time. If the Bible and the Christian doctrine has the solution to all these problems, why would my Christian Brother join a political party and preach about its doctrine?

On the other hand, if the Bible and the Christian doctrine has no solution to all these problems, then this cannot be a religion from God because God does not do half measures. Any religion, if it is a true religion, must provide men with answers and solutions to all of mans' problems; answers gives man confidence and comfort, that is why man finds comfort, satisfaction, and peace in Religion. However, if a man cannot find comfort, satisfaction or peace in his chosen religion, sooner or later, he will step out of that religion, either occasionally or permanently, in search of these sentiments elsewhere, such as in party politics, pagan rituals and corrupted traditions and secular cultures – and this is exactly when Satan takes advantage of him – and by 'Satan' I mean his own weaker self.

These New Age churches put more emphasis on material wealth than spiritual progress. Their leaders openly preach *Money* to the poor, and to the rich they preach *More Money*. Have they forgotten *Matthew 6 verse 24*? The sermon can become very uncomfortable to the less fortunate, and feel very uneasy to the pious, while to the rich and heartless it may be the best sermon to preach because his name might just become the title, he may be tagged a 'force to be reckoned with'. And even more sinister, this new so-called preaching is in fact motivational talks. These new preachers are in reality 'Motivational Speakers' and 'poets'. They deliver good talks, they are great in speech and hand gesture displays, and in their speeches or talks, or 'Sermons', they quote the biblical verses to support their statements. The Word of God has been reduced to a reference, and we call this wisdom, we call them wise, God-sent, Gods' messengers. They do not use their God-given wisdom to support the Word of God. They do not inform us how great and wise God is, they inform us how wise they are, but they are not wise. God does not make you stupid, you make yourself stupid; but it is God who makes you wise. And when God makes you wise, He does not intend you to prove to the world how much wiser you are, but rather how much Wiser He is. These 'pastors' represent themselves; they are fond of fame and praise. Instead of representing themselves to the people, they should be representing God to the people, and when the night comes, they should be going down on their knees representing the congregation to God; asking for its forgiveness and asking for guidance of the masses. This is a beautiful supplication.

Pastor Owen Makhado of *Divine Intervention Church* in Johannesburg, interviewed by *Move!* Magazine under the topic, *Has Sin Taken Over The Church?,* said:

"Pastors do not teach the message of holiness anymore because they fear that they might lose members and subsequently tithes and offerings. Because of greed, they overlook sin and grieve the Holy Spirit which should be the source of conviction". He goes on to say that "Today, pastors drive more expensive cars than the congregants they serve. The church has become a place to flaunt riches and success. Other churches even have ATM machines inside and some members pay their tithes via debit order. The best seats are reserved for the richest members who bring in tithes and offerings. The truth is, no amount of money can erase sin. It can buy you a fake relationship with a pastor, but never a relationship with God."

This is not a teaching of *"my religion is better than yours"*, this is a call back to the original teachings of *Jesus the son of Maria*. Whoever claims that his belief does not require *ubulungiswa* (correction) is misled. We say men got ego, but ego have gotten men, and it got us in its' grip. Until we free ourselves from all forms of ego and pride, we will become at ease with all of life – especially ourselves. Most of us may call these churches 'evolution' of the mainstream church, but honestly, is this not innovation?

This new age Christian Brother is, in essence, a Christianized socialite, or perhaps a de-Christianized believer, for his attitude has become worldly, his eyes are now glued on materialistic interests, most probably influenced by his liberal leader. However, out of all my beloved Brothers, this Brother, the Christian Brother, is the one I would love to work closely with, in terms of betterment of this beautiful country of ours. This is because we have the same vision, we share common goals, and, just like my Jewish Brother, he is closest to Islam. This Brother, my poor Christian Brother, if I would advise you, for counter-revolutionary reasons; I would recommend you back to the mainstream church, where you will wear a church uniform like the rest of the Brothers, with women covering their hair like they should. The church where ones' material wealth or fame has no place, nor relevance. A church where elders and knowledgeable men have more authority. Of course, I have no place in telling Christians what to do, and how to do it. I am a Muslim, I should worry about Muslim issues, shouldn't I? This is not a religious book and I am not a preacher. This book is about the Black man and his plight and solutions, whether one is Muslim, Christian, Hindu, Bahai' Faith, Buddhist, Rastafari, Jew or whichever faith. And since the majority of my Black South Afrikan Brethren are of the Christian faith, I had to focus on Christianity, so that we could get to the matter quicker and more effectively. However, I have to provide solutions as best as I can; applaud or condemn, it does not matter that much. What matters is seeing my Brothers free from ignorance and deceit. I want to see them escape the darkness of Satan and enter into the light of God. I want to see us win,

God Willing. I want us to recognize the wrath of false politics and experience the bliss of true Guidance. May God have mercy on us, may He guide us and make things easy for us in this life and in the Hereafter.

"For a time is coming when people will no longer listen to right teaching. They will follow their own desires and will look for teachers who will tell them whatever they want to hear".
– *2 TIMOTHY 4:3*

CHAPTER 7

My Political Brother

They cannot control wise men, and they cannot control rebels.

In this *Chapter*, we will focus mainly on the ANC (African National Congress), simply because today, it is both the ruling party and dominant party, and the longest existing political organization, which therefore makes it the party with most available historical political record. There is nothing extra special about the ANC as a liberation movement if it is to be compared with other Black liberation movements such as the PAC (Pan-Africanist Congress of Azania), the BC (Black Consciousness Movement of Azania), AZAPO (Azanian Peoples' Organization), and UDF (United Democratic Front).

My earliest full awareness of the ANC as a young child came when the announcements of the release of *Mr. Nelson*

Mandela hit the airwaves back in the late 80s. And when he was released in 1990, I was doing Grade 3, and I was eight years old. Everyone was cheering "*Mandela!*" – "*Mandela!*". But long before *Mandela's* release, where I am from, *Lamontville*, the ANC was dominant, and so active that homes of IFP (Inkatha Freedom Party) members and people who were suspected of being members or affiliated with the IFP, which was seen as the opposition Black party of so-called sell outs, were burnt down. I also learnt that the 'necklace' originated in *Lamontville*. 'Necklace' is a motor vehicle tyre placed around a persons' neck like an actual necklace, placed on the shoulders, and set alight. Those who were 'necklaced' were those suspected of being spies, spying either for the colonial white government, the police, or for the IFP.

I remember the lively streets of my neighborhood, filled with kids running around, playing *'street soccer'*, *'hide and seek, 'the tin', 'shumpu', 'magalobha', 'cops and robbers'*. We all wanted to be the *'robbers'*, the *'bad guys'*. We all wanted to play robbers; it represented the life we witnessed from the streets, our fathers, brothers and uncles were thug figures, and we admired the street power they possessed. On the other hand, the bad impression and first-hand experience we had with the police made their appearance unpleasant. We hated them – the police. They used to circle my hood in a *'hippo'* or the *'mellow yellow'* trucks. They would execute my Brothers either for being so-called criminals or for being politically active. Our fathers were jailed and killed, for either being dumb, or being smart. There was no way to win. The Apartheid government wanted the Black Brothers to be numb, just like zombies. They wanted them to be controllable. They understood that you cannot control an informed wise man and you cannot control an uninformed rebel with no cause. In essence, an uncontrollable wise man is in truth an informed rebel. Therefore, being politically-minded was the thing for most kids and teens. We didn't learn politics in schools, we learnt it first-hand in the township. We saw Brothers being hunted down day and night, chased, beaten down to death, and shot. This was back when we knew that the white man was our common enemy, today we've forgotten this, but nevertheless, today the white man still doesn't hate you because you are *ANC, IFP, AZAPO, EFF or PAC*; he hates you because you are

Black!

We will always obtain differing views on matters of politics and religion, and that we cannot change, but this exhibits the beauty of Black intellectualism; however, we should all work towards Black empowerment, in every form.

As a child born in the early 80s; 1982 to be exact, one of my legs is in the Apartheid era, the other one in the 'new free South Afrika'. My generation is the bridge between old folks and *'born-frees'*. We are mentally equipped for both regimes. During the freedom struggle, my Brothers had high hopes and visions; hopes that were big yet realistic. Brothers contemplated a free South Afrika that is free for every Black man; free in terms of the economy where Brothers would no longer have to work for the European settler in order to make a living. Free from poor education and poor medical care; a South Afrika free of selfish leaders and ruthless bureaucrats. A South Afrika that would be cultured and sovereign, as opposed to secular and godless. They dreamt of a South Afrika where everyone will be equal, respected and dignified. This is the dream that our Brothers and Sisters fought for, and died for. The concepts of 'equality' and 'ubuNtu' was not invented by *Nelson Mandela*, or the *ANC*. This concept was more than just a dream, it was a prayer inscribed in the hearts of Black freedom fighters and Black South Afrikans as a whole. After Mandela was released, we stopped contemplating, we now anticipated. He was made the number one contender for the first Black President but we know well that he was not the only one capable of this task, this must be clear; he was the most sold to the political Brother and un-politically conscious alike, he was the most advertised to the angry Brother, the hungry Brother, the Brother hungry for change, hungry for emancipation. But was he prepared for such a task? How was he fortified? How did he prepare for such a role of leading 49 million 'free men' when he had just gotten out of prison after 27 years? Who prepared him, both spiritually and mentally? Who and how? This is a very important question to ask. In her account, from a journal-orientated memoir called *491 Days, Prisoner number 1323/69,* Mama *Winnie Madikizela-Mandela* recalls:

"When I was in detention for all those months, my

two children nearly died. When I came out they were so lean; they had had such a hard time. They were covered in sores, malnutrition sores. And they (white people) wonder why I am like I am. And they have a nerve to say, 'Oh Madiba is such a peaceful person, you know. We wonder how he had such a wife who is so violent?' The (ANC) leadership on Robben Island was never touched; the leadership on Robben Island had no idea what it was like to engage the enemy physically. The leadership was removed (from the struggle) and cushioned behind prison walls; they had their three meals a day. In fact, ironically, we must thank the authorities for keeping our leadership alive; they were not tortured. They did not know what we were talking about and when we were reported to be so violent, engaged in the physical struggle, fighting the Boers underground, they did not understand because none of them had ever been subjected to that, not even Madiba himself – they never touched him, they would not have dared. We were the foot soldiers. We were their cannon fodder and it was us who were used as their political barometer each time they wanted to find out how the country was going to react. They tortured us knowing that it was going to leak to the country and they wanted to see the reaction. Tata (Madiba) could not comprehend how I had become so violent in the eyes of the police. They knew that I was involved in the military wing of the ANC and they knew I was a leader of the struggle underground. They knew I saved the soldiers who infiltrated into the country".

Now you ask yourself, does it befit a victor to be led by a prisoner of war, although he's a former? The men he was due to lead were of a different world, a different experience, even though he was one of them once upon a time, but they were now listening to a different kind of music, they were dancing a different dance, singing a different song. Intriguing indeed. But one thing we can all agree on: they were still hungry for liberation and freedom - a freedom where everyone is a shareholder, where everyone has a say, where everyone gains and enjoys a piece of the pie, and by *everyone* I mean Black people. Not a South Afrika that would be ran like a kingship, where only the *Mandelas*, the *Mbekis* or the *Zumas* would get all the privileges in the county's economic wealth, like having the best positions and best businesses, where only the *MK (Mkhonto Wesizwe)* guerillas, and the former exiled families would be a priority, a country where they would be evaluated by who and what they were during the struggle not what skills and ideas and ability they have to make this country progress. Everyone naively anticipated the end of poverty, cheap labor and slave labor. But then again, there are no rules in the game of deceit and no one is safe in the lion's den, not even the lion itself.

Ever since the ANC came into power, it has been telling us to calm down, integrate, and be obedient, and obviously be tolerant to the former invader colonists and racists, which is the very same thing that the Apartheid government forced us to do, except integrating (rather intermingling, only on their terms), and except that they came against us with guns, and the ANC came with a smile, a *Constitution*, and a *'Peace In Our Land'* dove - while the message is still the same. One young Black South Afrikan blogger wrote; *"We seek JUSTICE*

not revenge. No reconciliation without justice first. We can forgive
after compensation and JUSTICE has taken its course, not before".

The reality of the matter is that in our first free elections, the Black people of South Afrika did not vote for the ANC, the People voted for redistributive justice because we were sick and tired and angry and hopeful, yet, until this day, neither compensation nor justice has taken its course, and no one is fighting anymore because Black men flood the Parliament, the very same Black men whose responsibility is to enforce the justice we seek, the justice we are owed. Therefore, Black South Afrikans are still angry because compensation is still a pipe dream and justice has not been done. Conscious Blacks still hate whites, and whites do not know what to do because they are not running the show anymore (as it appears), but we know very well they are; they control minerals and the Reserve Bank for crying out loud. Black people are still waiting for the 'new South Afrika' that the late former president *Nelson Mandela* promised them, and it has been a long wait, 21 years, and is long overdue. The people do not care how much you know, they want to know how much you care. One thing the ruling party, the ANC, abundantly delivers is promises. Every speech delivered is nothing much more than a promise – giving Black people false hope. A radical yet constructive critique is seriously needed, not for hidden self-interest or ulterior motive but for betterment of this beautiful nation. Our country is not broke, it's only broken, and there is no power for Black people except in unity. We talk like this about the ANC not merely because it's the ruling party but because they are actually doing something, putting in work, and they should be, and we want them to do even more – they can do much better than this. We cannot waste our ink and voices talking about so-called Black-consciousness organizations that are all-talk and no action, whose new slogans are rooted in the blame-game and bitterness, instead of a new hope for a true and undying revolutionary nationalism and proper planning; therefore it would be a waste of our precious time. Yet we cannot ignore the ongoing deliberate political oppression imposed upon the radical pan-Afrikanist groups whose over a hundred Apartheid political prisoners are still incarcerated to this very day. The hypocrisy of the ruling party needs to be addressed, exposed and fought against as harshly, not because we want them out of leadership, for whoever takes over will not make any difference, rather because we want them to realize that we are aware of all that it does and we want them to correct all that requires correction; like those things that gave rise to *Julius Malema* and his party *EFF (Economic Freedom Fighters)*, an organization built upon a terribly flawed doctrine. *Julius Malema* – a young man who saw a loophole and took advantage, a low act that gave a prominent meaning to the saying *"In troubled times people don't look for the best rather the loudest"*. When one shouts over the poor and unorganized people, making all sorts of monetary promises, all logic stops because these people are hungry and desperate, but they are not stupid. The late great Ghanaian *President Kwame Nkrumah* said:

"We have a political problem. We must be politically organized, not economically organized. We have no economic problem, we are just politically unorganized. This is our only problem".

Truth is, the EFF is made up of angry and disappointed *ANC* and some PAC followers, and the ANC have no one to blame for this but themselves. And the root of this disappointment comes from the complete absence of pan-Afrikanism traits in its leadership. But how and why did we take this western imperialistic stance, , which legendary Kenyan writer *Ngugi Wa Thiong'o* described in his book *Decolonising the Mind:*

"The imperialist tradition in Africa is today maintained by the international bourgeoisie using the multinational and of course the flag-waving native ruling classes. The economic and political dependence of this African neo-colonial bourgeoisie is reflected in its culture of apemanship and parrotry enforced on a restive population through police boots, barbed wire, a gowned clergy and judiciary; their ideas are spread by a corpus of state intellectuals, the academic and journalistic laureates of the neo-colonial establishment".

Once members of our government learn that they are not royalty but leaders and the natives of this land, are not citizens but shareholders, because a citizen is *Isakhamuzi* (those who arrived, were welcomed, admitted into a dynasty, built homes and settled– the European, the Indian, and the Asian, not the Afrikan), I think their attitude will improve dramatically, positively. This whole condition of the Apartheid Caucasian government and Black government comparison kind of reminds me of what *Malcolm X* said during elections in the U. S., when he was asked who he favored between *Johnson* and *Goldwater*. He said:

> "I feel that as far as the American black man is concerned they are both just about the same. I feel that it is for the black man only a question of Johnson, the fox, or Goldwater, the wolf". He continues, "'Conservatism' in America's politics means 'Let's keep the niggers in their place'. And 'liberalism' means 'Let's keep the

kneegrows in their place – but tell them we'll treat them a little better; lets fool them more, with more promises'. With these choices, I felt that the American black man only needed to choose which one to be eaten by, the 'liberal' fox or the 'conservative' wolf – because both of them would eat him. I didn't go for Goldwater any more than for Johnson – except that in a wolf's den, I'd always know exactly where I stood; I'd watch the dangerous wolf closer than I would the smooth, sly fox. The wolf's very growling would keep me alert and fighting him to survive, whereas I might be lulled and fooled by the tricky fox." He adds, "Goldwater flatly told the black man he wasn't for them – and there is this to consider: always, the black people have advanced further when they have seen they have to rise up against a system that they clearly saw outright was against them. Under the steady lullabies sung by foxy liberals, the Northern Negro became a beggar. But the Southern Negro, facing the honestly snarling white man, rose up to battle the white man for his freedom – long before it happened in the North." Adding to that he wrote; "If it had been Goldwater, all I am saying is that the black people would at least have known they were dealing with an honestly growling wolf, rather than a fox who could have them half-digested before they even knew what was happening".

The same thing applies to the Black man's plight in South Afrika today; with the Apartheid government we knew exactly that we were dealing with the devil, and we had to take up arms and face him, but with the new government we are dealing with a serpent, a devil in disguise, a deceiver, who came as a friend, a Brother – the kind of Brother who eats in front of you and tells you, *"this is progress therefore be grateful because at least one of us is eating"*, and tells you to be patient because your day is coming too; a friend who will not share with you. This Brother, instead, rather dines with his open enemy. His enemy of yesterday is today his best friend and ally, and his long time true Brother and comrade, the Black masses of South Afrika and entire Afrika is, today, neglected, forgotten, and left to fend for herself.

"In the name of forgiveness and reconciliation between old enemies, Mandela lapped up all sugary citations and praises heaped on him by the western media. Once the memory of Robben Island faded, he befriended the Queen of England. He dined with Margaret Thatcher, an unrepentant supporter of apartheid in its violent form. And to add insult to an injury, Thatcher bundled her wayward son, Mark, to Cape Town, a new world, free from apartheid, which she championed with iron zeal!"

"Mandela's clarion call for justice and equality between the races has exploded in his face. Architects, propagators, collaborators and perpetrators of the worst apartheid atrocities against blacks are still sitting pretty on the hills of Sandton, Johannesburg and Cape Town sipping chilled champagne and caviar". Extract from *Nigerian Muse* article by Tijani. The writer concludes, painfully: "Mandela's South Africa favored the mass immigration of whites not blacks. Nigeria, which played an admirable role in the darkest period of South Africa's struggle for emancipation, had a raw deal under Mandela. We are not accorded any special relationship. Indeed, Nigerians were labeled and caricatured as dope dealers and 419ers, while Mark Thatcher and other scions of apartheid lovers were welcomed with golden carpets!"

The government hypocrisy in this part of the world is impossible to ignore, it has to be addressed. We see whites operating freely in illegal arms dealings, brothel businesses and drug trade, and every day we see (Black) street venders treated like criminals. We see South Afrika, a former colonized country working hand-in-hand with current colonizers, Israel, an Apartheid state. How can a Black man believe in a system that is not designed for him to succeed – a system that rather gives opportunities to Chinese over her own youth. Now who can still deny that the Black man in leadership is just a face with no voice? In scrutinization of the condition of a Black man, one learns that in actuality, the Black man is a conditioned man. Therefore, I am not surprised to find that my poor political Brother is blind to these facts. He is blind to these facts because he supports an individual or party, he is not a supporter of Justice. He is not a supporter of Truth. He is not a supporter of the Black people. He follows the party fiercely; he reads about it in the tabloids, in books. He watches the News and he is assured that he knows exactly what is going on, but he is clueless. Any information or ideas opposing his trusted party or leader, he rejects without a trial. He does not research what he hears and reads, and when confronted with new information he bluntly attacks the writer, which in the end exposes his ignorance. And who is a greater example of this fact than *Julius Malema*, who once verbally crushed everyone that opposed *President* Jacob Zuma's leadership, who once loved *President Jacob Zuma* enough to die for him, and then hated him enough to kill him himself. Truth be told, from the word *GO!*, the ANC government since the Mandela regime has failed dismally in some of the most important social issues, even in the matters of elementary human needs such as housing, as described by *Nigel C. Gibson*:

"Progress in addressing the post-apartheid housing 'crisis' is often counted by the number of houses delivered. Even if this number is below what is needed (which it is), and even if it is a well-built house (which it most certainly isn't), and large enough to accommodate a family (which it certainly isn't), and built in an area close to amenities and jobs (again no), the fact is that a house is seen as a major step forward for the 'beneficiary' of housing, while at times it might be a calamity for the poor." He continues; "The poor have no say because they are not seen as 'stakeholders'. The poor are not stakeholders because they do not count; they are quite simply a subjugated mass that can only be represented. Thus they count only

> as vote banks at election times, but even then
> they are counted numerically as substance, and
> not taken into account as political subjects
> (which is why when they organize, the poor
> are considered 'out of order')."

Our townships are 'projects', built on 'trial and error'. The so-called community development is in actual fact a monopolized corporation, a one-man economic enrichment. Again, my dear political Brother is blind to this clear fact. But we have to feel for him and understand that a hypnotized person cannot rationalize. He is so blind that he, himself, might be living in one of these one-room, two-room RDP houses with no yard, located in a gutter, yet he will still deny this, instead he will shift the blame to the so-called tender owners. However, who are these tender owners? Aren't they the ANC politicians, or their relatives and friends? Wake up Brother! This discussion is not even about the ANC, again, it is about you, the Black man. It is about us as Black people of *Azania*, a *promised land*. If any ruling party is not helping in eradicating basic plights of the People such as joblessness then it must get out of the way, no matter who the ruling party is. There is no time for playing favorites, our people are dying in despair. This is less than what we hoped for, fought for, and died for, therefore we cannot be quiet. The men who came to lead us were either in prison or in exile – how did they come to lead 'ordinary' men who had no time for negotiations with the oppressor, men who were in the battleground day and night fighting the enemy, fighting for their lives and protection of their families? People need to understand that, just like the business world and marketing, the government is nothing without its intelligence agency. If, for example, an insurance advertisement says, you will pay *'only R99,99 per month'*, immediately your mind says: "Wow! It's *less* than a R100, great deal", yet it is only 1 cent you are saving, which really is nothing. It is all a mind game – the mind-game that is played by the white-owned media like *SABC* and *eTV* when they repeatedly broadcasts a documentary on Apartheid so that you cry your eyes out and thank God for the ANC and accept or at least overlook whatever nonsensical business is going on in the leadership because "at least things have changed", so you say. It is the same mind game when you hear words such as, *''The People Shall Govern''*, or *"Our Constitution"*, words like *"Democracy"*, *"Concerned Citizen"*, *"Rainbow Nation"*, *"Proudly South African"*, *"Correctional Services"* and *"Correctional Facility"*. All these are oxymoronic words, they are not real, they were created to dumb you down so that you would play along without any suspicion. But if you take some time out and really think about these terms then look at the situation, without a doubt you will see how you have been fooled, and for how long, and of course for what reason. The reason is your support and/or participation. Brothers today sell their souls to the ANC politicians, everyone hustles for an ANC membership card, their excuse being that it will open doors for them in the business and entertainment sectors. Truthfully speaking, South Afrika has not seen revolution yet. Since the beginning, since 1994, the ANC government never brought revolution; instead, the ANC government revamped the White System, the Apartheid System. Revolution is not wordplay, revolution is action; revolution is real change. You cannot name a road after a revolutionary and say you have honored him, or name a bridge, a school, or a stadium or whatever. You can only honor a revolutionary by applying his doctrine, ideas, and his principles in your leadership in the system. Until South Afrika is *economically* for all South Afrikans, not only Indians, Europeans and Chinese, *Robert Sobukwe* will remain dishonored and unrecognized. Until the Black race is taken seriously, and esteemed, and given high status through housing, education, and business, while being treated equally, not according to ones relationship with any party politicians, *Steve Biko* will remain dishonored and unrecognized in the eyes of the system. And as long as these two great men are not honored, we haven't seen Justice, and what is Revolution without Justice!

There are millions of proud, selfless, and brave South Afrikans who literally gave their all for the liberation of this country from the claws of colonialism, some lost their spouses, others children, parents, and friends, education, security, identity, and others lost their lives. Today they are sitting looking at what this country has become in comparison to what it should have became, and they are disgusted!

"People who had given everything, wonder, with their empty hands and bellies, as to the reality of their victory". Said *Frantz Fanon*. It was even more like he was talking about the Black elite in the ANC government when he said; *"The people find out the iniquitous fact that exploitation can wear a black face."*

Political failure is almost traditional in this country, where past and present rulers are as identical, except for skin tan, shape of their noses and size of their lips. Let us be reminded that, the *Democratic Alliance (DA)*, which is made up of *National Party* and *Democratic Party*, not so long ago, was pro-Apartheid. The DA did not only openly support racism, Apartheid, and oppression of Black people but also took part in it, playing a major role in the mass brutal killings of Black people, innocent men, harmless women, and defenseless children. It does not concern me whether the DA has changed and adopted a new agenda or not, whether they put a Black man in leadership or not, whether they publicly apologize to Black people or not, my concern is with the ANC not DA, because I do not recognize the DA, as they have never ever been a freedom fighting party, but rather a pro-white, anti-Black, *Nazist* organization. They say keep your friends close and your enemies closer, and the DA have done exactly that by putting a Black man in leadership, and most of you Black folk are like a mouse chasing the cheese mindless of the trap. A leader is judged by the organization he represents, and the organization is judged by it's ideology. *Mmusi Maimane* is the unmasked face of white rule. He is a modern-day monument of Apartheid memorial. He is a Black man representing a white group with a white agenda, he is standing on the shoulders of Apartheid architects and white supremacist giants. He married a white woman – he has no interest whatsoever in changing the condition of a Black man. The ANC, on the other hand, indirectly, took over where the *National Party* left off – corning, cunning, aggressive, selfish, bureaucratic and autocratic.

In an ideal land, corruption in leadership is as evil as the white man himself. Hosting the *Rugby World Cup* tournament twice made no difference, hosting the first *Soccer World Cup* in Afrika did not change the price of bread for the better, it did not change my taxi fare; instead, the West, the settlers, and former colonists made billions, and the indigenous remained where they are supposed to be, in poverty. Looking back to all these twenty one years of 'free South Afrika', very little has changed, and these little changes are always seen just when the elections are about to take place – tricknology is corruption itself.

"… China, a country where industrial development has lifted 600 million people out of absolute poverty within 30 years. China, it should be pointed out, is highly corrupt. Despite its many 'bad apples' at all levels of government it has nevertheless achieved GDP growth of almost 10 percent a year, year in, year out, for over 30 years. This proves beyond all doubt that corruption does not necessarily prevent rapid development. The reason for China's success is because its government acts in the interest of China, not of the West. Its bad apples might be corrupt, but they cannot be paid to follow orders from abroad."- Vijay Mehta in *The Economics of Killing*.

In his book *Islam and the Third Universal Theory*, *Mahmoud Ayoub* refers to the late Brother Leader *Mu'ammar Gaddafi* who regarded this so-called Democratic system as a false Democracy, and considered party politics as 'an abortion of (true) Democracy', saying: *"If, for example, 51 percent of the population votes for someone and 49 percent voted against him, then 49 percent of the people would be denied their right to be represented by someone acceptable to them. Gaddafi, moreover, regards election campaigns as a form of demagoguery because only the rich can enter them"*.

Now this is where the *"Most High Constitution"* comes in, I'm talking about *"Divine Guidance"*. Most of our political organizations have no spiritual foundation, their 'clever' words may tickle your ears but they hardly touch the soul or cultivate the mind. I respect Black consciousness movements because they are built upon spirituality, they have 'religious' grounds. One can easily be a Muslim and a Black nationalist at the same time. The Koran says, *"Oh! Mankind, We have created you male and female and made you into nations and tribes that you may know one another"* (49:13). Now how can we know one another without Knowledge of Self, without proper knowledge of our nationhood? If one cannot love another person without loving themselves, then as nations we cannot live in peace and harmony if we do not promote peace and harmony amongst our own people first.

However, having an ideal ideology will not get you anywhere as an organization or movement if you are not both organized and mobilized. I wish to see, in the near future, organizations such as PAC, BCM and AZAPO becoming more visible in our communities, more accessible, more influential and ultimately dominant, not because we are in need of party politics, but because our youth has been systematically pushed away from self-determining political aspirations and swiftly seduced into a charismatic imperial bourgeoisie whose members are not moved by a socialist agenda that binds all people of all races and class under the banner of love and progress, but rather aroused by individualistic maximum profit, regardless. We have designed for our youth a culture of selfishness. The ruins of the *Black Power* edifice of hope rests in the dust beneath our feet like the breathless body of *Steve Biko*. Who is to blame: the killers of *Comrade Chris Hani* who were not even his enemies or his close acquaintances and allies who have abandoned his noble cause for personal material desires? I place no blame or judgment upon any man whose weaknesses may be my strengths and whose strengths may be my weaknesses. Some other political Brethrens of mine joined unions and communist parties, hoping for a true and honest *Che Guevara* type of leadership. To their surprise, there was no such thing. This is politics! If a true leader is not yet dead, he is badmouthed in the press or is somewhere in the gutter suppressed and unrecognized. The so-called workers unions, today, are affiliated and taking orders from the right wing *above*, then go back to the man *down* there to soften him with empty promises. His first duty is to keep the poor man *down there* angry, his second duty is to keep him immobile, unless and until orders from *up above* say *"unleash"*. Strange enough, these so-called communists are affiliated with parties who not only have nothing to do with Communism and Socialism but also who are enemies of Communist ideology. Communism in this country, and almost in every part of the world, is dead. In this country, *SACP (South African Communist Party)* leaders support this governments' imperialism in it's most unguarded fascism, and this is because they also are part of this 'new' empire. These once devoted Communist leaders now live in upper-class suburbs with electric fences hiding from the poor and dangerous, they wine and dine with the rich in 'high places', they are celebrities living posh lifestyles, the same lavish life lived by Capitalists disguised as Democrats. Only when a rally happens do they visit the rural area, the township, the slum village, the gutter, to organize the hopelessly ignorant and poor Black people who need nothing but a *Slogan* t-shirt, a matching cap, and a good speech to become all *fired up* and ready to hit the street in furious rage. How cheap my highly-spirited people have become. It's embarrassing! I am not fighting against anyone, this should be stated again and again; I am only a Black man fighting for himself – fighting for his self-determination, his right to liberty; his right to being. If negative racism and classism wears a Black face, we shall still fight it, and with the same enthusiasm and aggression as we did when it wore a white face. We should not even be discussing or arguing about this. The fact that we are, is an insult to *Z.K Matthews*, *Anton Lembede*, *Robert Sobukwe* and *Steve Biko* – these are easily the most influential South Afrikan liberation fighters of all time. It is never my muse to come as opposition to another Black Brother like myself, when we should be on the same side discussing further progress for the Black man. Unfortunately, this country is once again ran by *ogombela kwesakhe* and coming across as seemingly against them is treated as treason. These shots are not personalized against anyone, we are not fighting certain individuals or groups, we are merely fighting against hypocrisy, or rather that which seems hypocritical. The Black man needs to organize, let us bring it back to the community where the real struggle is, not in parliament. No matter what organization one belongs to, we don't care about any of that, we have an urgent and common goal – to see the Black man progress; and this time we shall go up together hand-in-hand. When the people have been put down for so long, being down becomes normal and acceptable until getting back up doesn't even cross their minds. *RISE BLACK MAN RISE!*

May the Almighty God make us be among those who spread love and peace, may He open our eyes and our hearts, making us love our Black selves and follow the slogan, *"Race*

First!"

"True leadership demands complete subjugation of self, absolute honesty, integrity and uprightness of character, courage and fearlessness and, above all consuming love for one's people." – Robert Mangaliso Sobukwe

CHAPTER 8

My Millitary Brother

The Masses will always laugh at Supreme Knowledge, because Supreme understanding is never given to the masses

These are the protectors of the country and we can see clearly that they are fierce patriots. They are ready and willing to lay their precious and valuable lives down and die for this country. They are doing all this for the People, the citizens. Now the most important question is, what are they protecting the country or the People from – from poverty, from joblessness, from financial exploitation, such as our corrupt banking system and interests rates? If the answer is

Yes, then why we do not see any changes. If the answer is No, then, really, what are they protecting us from? Or maybe the right question is not 'what', but rather 'who'? Who are they protecting us against? *China, America, Libya,* or maybe *England*? We know that China is one of the leading importers in this country. Moreover, they have enough power to determine who enters this country and who doesn't; as they did with the *Dalai Lama*. We know that it definitely is not America. America is our social and judicial role model; if they do it in America; we *have* to do it here too – from political influence to the television shows such as *Pop Idols, Big Brother, The Apprentice, South Africa's Got Talent, Dancing with the Stars,* etc. We watch their TV shows, play their music, sell their magazines, wear their fashion, and talk their slang with their accent. Literally, we are Afrikans chasing the American dream, which *Black America* itself hasn't realized. Therefore, we can rest assured it is not America we are being protected against. Could it be Libya? Actually, it could be Libya; we do not trade with Libya, instead, we trade with the enemies of Libya. We never had Libyan Leader *Colonel Gaddafi*, like *Barack Obama*, coming into this country to deliver open public talks, sharing his wisdom and knowledge and this is the greatest modern-day Leader Afrika had, and our half-Black/half-white brother *Barack Obama* and his friends killed him and Black Brothers in South Afrika cheered upon this act, now we have no one, and I mean no one who is willing to die for the people of Afrika in the name of Justice. His ideas are not as wide spread even though he proved himself selfless when it came to Afrikan political liberation and self-realization. I wonder if the military Brother knows anything about loyalty: for loyalty is not the following of the rules but the following of the righteous path. In *Gaddafi's* words;

"Let the free people of the world know that we could have bargained over and sold out our course in return for a personal and stable life." He continued: "We received many offers to this effect but we chose to be the vanguard of the confrontation as a badge of duty and honor. Even if we do not win immediately, we will give a lesson to future generations that choosing to protect the nation is an honor and selling it out is the greatest betrayal that history will remember forever despite the attempts of others to tell you otherwise."

However, we know it is not Libya, nor is it England. The reality of the matter, is that the military and the police are not to protect the People, but rather to serve the government and to protect the government against any foreign regime change attempt and against the uprising of its own People; protection against any form of rebellion which may lead to treason or revolution. The police is indeed a private political army and such a country is called a "Police State". A soldier and a police officer ask no questions, he has no right to think for himself, let alone act for himself. Do you remember the *Marikana* massacre not so long ago? Have you forgotten how police mercilessly massacred our Black Brothers, their own Black Brothers too? He, the military Brother, is indeed a puppet on a string. He has been lied to; they told him to love his country, and therefore serve his country, but he is being deceived. He is definitely not serving in the interest of the People, but rather of the bigger white racist and evil elite, whose mission is to control the world by deceit through media and military force, in preparation for the manifestation of the Great Fall of Mankind. This elite controls clueless Black politicians who sold their souls for monetary wealth and fame. The masses will always laugh at supreme knowledge, because supreme understanding is never given to the masses.

I remember that as a small boy I had a great army of toy soldiers that my grandmother bought me. We were not living together at the time, my grandmother and I, so in order to keep me visiting her on every school holiday, she kept all my toys with her, and I could not take them to Lamontville with me, where I lived with my mother. Every time my school closed I would go on visits to my grandmother in *Mayville* so that I could play with my toy army. It was something I greatly looked forward to. At that point in my life maybe I wanted to grow up and become a soldier, all young boys did, perhaps because soldiers have status, power, and most importantly the license to kill. To a young boy, this means a lot. Boys and men alike adore power. Then, growing up, we were fed American army movies such as *Delta Force, Dirty Dozen,* and many others, which we enjoyed very much, also which I now understand as a mental preparation for Western occupation of the Arab world. American soldiers, in these block busters, were always the 'good guys', the 'saviors', and the Muslim Arab soldiers were always the 'evil bunch', the villains. This was to prepare the masses and buy them into American support against the Islamic nations, whose intention was nothing but occupation and control. Today these type of movies are made into sitcoms and romantic stories. Still the Muslim is ridiculed. American actor, *Ben Affleck* once said, *"The way people speak about Arabs and Muslims would not be tolerated if the same things were said about Jews".* In the holy bible, we read stories about a Jewish boy, a heroic figure named *Samson* killing thousands of Palestinians. Similar stories are told about Blacks, where God defeated a million Ethiopian men labeled 'the enemy' *(2 Chronicles 12:9-12),* and the so-called *Curse of Ham* is associated with the Black race by Western bible scholars. These are the foundations of hate, racism, slavery, brutality, and colonialism, blueprinted in the form of a so-called religious scripture by those who wrote books with their own hands and said, *"This is from God"*. My dislike for the soldiers began when I encountered real soldiers around my neighborhood. These now were no longer my toy army, these were real soldiers, with real ammunition, shooting with real bullets, doing real killings, and these killings were of our real Brothers. I remember I was still in lower primary then, about five or six years old. There was a period, called the *'State of Emergency'*, with police brutality and military killings of Black youth, even school children that left a lot of them dead. Since then I have learnt that whenever there is a white governance there is also a need for revolution. My poor military Brothers, policemen included, believe that they are doing service and justice to the people and the state, they do not realize that the People and the state are two entities on different ends. When the state is happy the People are not, when the People are happy the state is not. The soldier serving the state believes he is in essence serving the people, but the truth of the matter proves otherwise.

On Sunday 20 May, 2012, thousands of veterans of the Iraqi

and Afghanistan wars led a peace march in Chicago at the site of the largest NATO summit in the organization's six-decade history. This march marked the largest protest in the weeklong series of actions against the NATO summit. Soldiers let their voices be heard as they returned their medals one by one from the stage. Veterans of wars of NATO walked up to the stage and told the crowds why they chose to return their medals to NATO. Here are a few of the statements made by these brave ex-military veterans (extracts from *Al-Ummah* magazine, Rajab 1433 AH issue):

"My name is Greg Miller. I'm a veteran of the United States Army infantry with service in Iraq 2009. The military hands out cheap tokens like this to soldiers, service members, in an attempt to fill the void where their conscience used to be once they indoctrinate it out of you. But that didn't work on me, so I'm here to return my Global War on Terrorism Medal, and my National Defense Medal, because they're both lies."

"My name is Shawna Foster, and I was a nuclear biological chemical specialist for a war that didn't have any weapons of mass destruction. So I deserted. I'm one of 40,000 people that left the United States Armed Forces because this is a lie!"

"My name is Zach LaPorte, and I'm an Iraq war veteran from Milwaukee, Wisconsin. Thank you. I'm giving back my medal today because I was duped into an illegal war that was sold to me on the guise that I was going to be liberating the Iraqi people, when instead of liberating the people; I was liberating their oil fields."

"My name is Vince Emanuele, and I served with the United States Marine Corps. First and foremost, this is for the people of Iraq and

Pakistan. Second of all, this is for our real forefathers. I'm talking about the Student Nonviolent Coordinating Committee. I'm talking about the Black Panthers. I'm talking about the civil rights movements. I'm talking about unions. I'm talking about our socialist brothers and sisters, our communist brothers and sisters, our anarchist brothers and sisters, and our ecology brothers and sisters. That's who our real forefathers are. And lastly – and most importantly – our enemies are not 7000 miles from home. They sit in boardrooms. They are CEOs. They are bankers. They are hedge fund managers. They do not live 7000 miles away from home. Our enemies are right here, and we look at them every day. They are not the men and women who are standing on this police line. They are the millionaires and billionaires who control this planet, and we've had enough of it. So they can take their medals back."

Another military veteran named *Chuck Winant* stood on behalf of *"six good Americans who really wanted to be here but they couldn't be. They couldn't be, because when they came to the U. S. border, they'd be immediately arrested. And the crime they'd be arrested for was refusing to continue to participate in the crimes against the people of Iraq and Afghanistan."* He continued saying that these good Americans who are exiled now from this country deserve amnesty.

There are not only soldiers and sergeants who refused redeployment, but also members of higher rankings. A similar event took place as well in 1971 outside the U. S. Capitol staged by Vietnam Veterans.

Frederick the Great, King of Prussia, who was very much praised for his military excellence, once said: *"If my soldiers were to begin to think, not one would remain in the ranks."* However, today, more and more, day in and day out, soldiers are seeing the light, they are realizing the truth about the wars they have been sent to fight, as another American soldier named *Mike Prysner* said: *"We are told we are fighting terrorists. The real terrorist was me. And the real terrorism is this occupation."*

These are but a few of the activities by the 'Civilized World' which was not only built on slave labor but still continues to enslave and slaughter people of other parts of the world which, strangely enough, always happen to be people of darker complexion! Never once have I heard of a white 'dictator' or white 'terrorist', or at least a 'Christian' one. Even white Christians such as *Hitler* and *Mussolini* were never given such tags.

A soldier, by very nature, is a man machine, made by man to protect a certain Man from certain men. A soldier is in no way going to protect you from a natural event, or any social ills such as financial inadequacy of the people, but rather, from political uprising. Take note; I said *protect*. He cannot protect people from an earthquake, which is beyond his control, but he can protect a man from attack. Therefore, his military strength is physical, and he can only fight off the physical man. Moreover, he is trained to perform rather than think. His duty is limited to the performance of the task at hand, tasks given to him. He is not asked to, nor expected to, scrutinize these assignments. When having to exercise his mental ability he has to, of course, think along military lines (the guidelines, protocols, and orders) which at the end proves he is not thinking for and by himself.

In *Decolonising the Mind,* legendary Kenyan writer *Ngugi Wa Thiong'o* writes:

> "Imperialism, led by the USA, presents the struggling peoples of the earth and all those calling for peace, democracy and socialism with the ultimatum: accept theft or death".

We live in a world where, in the words of British MP, Brother *George Galloway, "the victims of terrorism are called the terrorists, and the terrorists are called the victims of terrorism".* There are a number of reports of American soldiers and journalists who went to Iraq and Afghanistan to perform their allotted duties and instead converted to Islam. They departed from their countries with hearts burning from anger and hate, for they were misled into believing that Muslims are the enemies of Democracy and Liberation, most of all, enemies of America and all other so-called civilized and Christian nations. However, their experience when in close and personal contact with these people of predominantly Islamic descent, turned out to be completely the opposite from what they had been taught. This is purely because when you engage with any human being on a personal and human level, without fail you will meet a human being, both in you and in the other man or woman. While your being meets the other being, God's being becomes highly visible because it is not your eyes that are opening but your heart. And this is why eventually, the perpetrator is always regretful and the victim is always forgiving. I'm mentioning this because the SADF (South African Defence Force) is also, at times, deployed to fight in this World War 3 'Arab Spring', Muslim occupation. Funnily enough, in all these political wars, Religion is the order of the day. Every shot fired, every bomb exploded, and every breath taken, is blamed on religious conflict. But why does religion have such a bad name? In South Afrika and Afrika as a whole, our problems, in our violent political history caused by colonization, were resolved in churches and mosques. *Alik Shahadah*, on the article *War Myth And Religion*, wrote:

> "Patterns of human conflict cannot be mapped to degrees of religiosity. Yet, in the Western discourse, religion is absolutist, divisive, irrational, brainwashing, the cause of slavery, the cause of war, the cause of strife, wasted wealth and time. As *Kwame Ture* said because Europe then has this conflict with religion, they make the issues of Europe the concern of the world. So what is true for Europeans must be by default be true for everyone else. And finally in the case of Islam "preaches a culture of hate."

And what does all this have to do with my Black Brother in the military? When forcibly required to fight in the Vietnam

War, *Muhammad Ali,* the legendary Boxer, refused unapologetically at a press conference in front of government officials. He said *"Why should they ask me to put on a uniform and go ten thousand miles from home and drop bombs and bullets on brown people in Vietnam while so-called Negro people in America are treated like dogs."* He added: *"If I thought going to war would bring freedom and equality to 22 million of my people, they wouldn't have to draft me, I'd join tomorrow."* Immediately after this he was banned from boxing until he made an appeal after three years. When he was asked whether he would join the army if his appeal failed, he said *"My prayers, my sacrifice, my life and my death are all for Allah. So I don't see why I should break the rules of my faith and I have no quarrel with the Vietnamese."*

Therefore, we should ask the Black South Afrikan soldier fighting wars organized by *United Nations*, America and NATO, if he could list a few, just a few changes which these wars he fought have contributed to the economic, political and social progress of his people, if there are any. While you are out there, in a life and death situation, fighting in the interest of white billionaires behind closed curtains, is your

Mama back home becoming some sort of an *'-illionaire'* as well? Is your family protected from hunger and police brutality? Does the future look bright to you? Are you satisfied by how things are in this country, in this world? Are you proud of yourself? Of course, you are one of the few who are lucky enough to get a job in this country, and I understand how difficult it is for you to risk chances of losing it, but we cannot sell our souls for money, or comfort, or anything of this world. We cannot sell our souls for what a man can offer; because what a man can offer, another man can as well, and, tragically, another man can take away. But what God can offer, no man can, and no man can take away. Not too far from a religious call; however, it is not. This is a call to consciousness and emancipation of the Black mind; within it we come into remembrance that 'God' is not a name, it's a natural position and divine status. But what does this job entail? Does it not blind, or perhaps brainwash the Black man and lead him into partaking in Black-on-Black killings? We live in a country where it is okay for policemen to kill people. However, it is not difficult to see that the people killed are the Blacks as though they are actually targeted. Is it because they are criminals, killers, or are they killed simply because they are inferior or weak? No matter what the case may be, the fact remains that the police are as corrupt as the criminals they kill. To guide you from being sidetracked, I have to remind you that this Chapter is about the Black military Brother not his victims, who are always Black like himself; it is about why and what leads him into believing that it is okay to pull a trigger against his own Brother and feel no remorse about it, but rather call this a patriotic act. Has he traded Brotherhood for Patriotism? Even us as civilians, we see absolutely nothing sinister about this picture until it happens to the one close to us. Whether these killings are justified in the Criminal Court (in which they always are) or not, we have to re-establish our sense of *family* as the Black Tribe. We live in a country where if you are a Black male, being on the street is not safe for you; where you run from your 'hustler Brother' and get shot down by your 'military Brother', for any reason.

When *Frantz Fanon* writes about *The Pitfalls of National Consciousness*, it seems as if he is talking about the MK (Mkhonto Wesizwe), the military wing of the ANC:

"After independence, the party sinks into an extraordinary lethargy. The militants are only called upon when so-called popular manifestations are afoot, or international conferences, or independence celebrations. The local party leaders are given administrative posts, the party becomes an administration, the militants disappear into the crowd and take the empty title of citizen. Now that they have fulfilled their historical mission of leading the bourgeoisie to power, they are firmly invited to retire so that the bourgeoisie may carry out *its* mission in peace and quiet. But we have seen that the national bourgeoisie of under-developed countries is incapable of carrying out any mission whatever. After a few years, the break-up of the party becomes obvious, and any observer, even the most superficial, can notice that the party, today the skeleton of its former self, only serves to immobilize the people. The party, which during the battle had drawn to itself the whole nation, is falling into pieces. The intellectuals who on the eve of independence rallied to the party, now make it clear by their attitude that they gave their support with no other end in view than to secure their slices of the cake of independence. The party is becoming a means of private advancement. There exists inside a new regime, however, an inequality in the acquisition of wealth and in monopolization. Some have double sources of income and demonstrate that they are specialized in opportunism. Privileges multiply and corruption triumphs, while morality declines. Today the vultures are too numerous and too voracious in proportion to the lean spoils of the national wealth. The party, a true instrument of power in the hands of the bourgeoisie, reinforces the machine, and ensures that the people are hemmed in and immortalized. The party helps the government to hold the people down. It becomes more and more clearly antidemocratic, an implement of coercion. The party is objectively, sometimes subjectively, the accomplice of the merchant bourgeoisie. In the same way that the national bourgeoisie conjures away its phase of construction in order to throw itself into the enjoyment of its wealth, in parallel fashion in the institutional sphere it jumps the parliamentary phase and chooses a dictatorship of the national-socialist type".

When former president *Nelson Mandela* was in power, he urged all South Afrikan citizens to bring forward each and every firearm they had, and people did just that in large numbers, and from then police brutality and killings of these defenseless citizens escalated, and these killings were only directed at Black people. When *Bheki Cele*, former South African Police Commissioner came into power he said the same and waited for the right time, then ordered his policemen *"shoot to kill!"*, and again it was Black people killed. In 1933, *Adolf Hitler*, the most renowned mass murderer of the intruder Jews said *"To conquer a nation, first disarm its citizens"*. Have we been tricked by Black men we trusted? Have we being hypnotized by good speeches? Now, which Brother can be hypocritical and say we do not, as Black Brothers, need weaponry to protect ourselves from these evil machines, these *man-made* beasts? *Dr Amos Wilson* wrote:

> "Cultural continuity is maintained by educating children in the ways of their culture. And they are educated in the ways of their culture to MAINTAIN their culture, to advance its interests; and ultimately to try to maintain its very survival. That is the fundamental reason people are educated. What does it matter if you learn physics or computer science and everything else and you cannot defend yourself against a military assault by Europeans or a germ warfare assault? A knowledge of computer science, a knowledge of law, a knowledge of all these other things matters not at all if you are unable to use that

knowledge for your self defense. And as long as we are not educated to defend ourselves against these people then we are being incorrectly educated. Nothing else matters".

Therefore, self-defense should be the priority, not because we want to escalate the situation, which may be the case, but simply as a means of survival. If we do not fight back, then we are not doing justice to ourselves. May God make killings distasteful and ugly for everyone, and make forgiveness preferable and peace prevail.

In remembrance of *Thamsanqa "Mordecai" Mdima*, a young Lamontville hero killed by police during "state of emergency", *Sbu Mkhize*, a young Lamontville fearless revolutionary killed by the Apartheid army. This is for *Mgcineni "Mambush" Noki*, shot dead by South African police along with 44 others and 78 injured during the *Lonmin* strike, a mine workers protest; *Andries Tatane* who was brutally killed by police during a service delivery protest in Ficksburg. All this we shall never forget! This is for all police victims whose only crime was Blackness; from *George Jackson*, younger brother *Jonathan Jackson*, *Fred Hampton*, to *Eric Garner*, *Tamir Rice*, *Mike Brown*, *Freddie Gray*, and millions of others.

CHAPTER 9

My Celebrity Brother

We are being told what and what not to like

ollywood, the *'Dream Machine'*. This Brother is the most looked up to, and if endorsed well, he can even be more influential than a nations' political leaders combined. This Brother is a trendsetter by profession, or more accurately, *Trance-Setter*. In the past, celebrities were media personnel, musicians, actors, and sport personalities, but times have changed. Today the list of types of celebrities is endless. We have celebrity doctors, scientists, journalists, politicians, pastors, chefs, bloggers, paparazzi, magazine and newspaper editors, etc. What are the makings of a celebrity? First, he or she must have a career, then, must be on television, magazines and/or newspapers. He must be famous for something, however, nowadays the doing *nothing* has become the *doing* – which can get one famous. Since we have singers singing about drugs and alcohol and sex, and TV stars playing 'bad guy' characters, South Afrikan media have made it very clear that celebrities are to be celebrated for anything, whether good or bad, positive or negative. On television, you are told what and what not to like, who to and who not to like, what to eat, what to wear, how to talk. Our children are practically raised by television, while we practically raise them according to how the media say we should. Television shows such as *Generations* told us to accept homosexuality; our Traditional system and our holy Books do not accept homosexuality, but *Generations* told us to forget our holy Books and customs and accept it, and we did. *Live* (the music show) tells us what kind of music and songs we must like. On TV and magazines, each season, we are being told what to wear, and even how to wear it.

As a child, fascinated by movies and television shows, like every other child, I had my television heroes. Even though the likes of *Jean-Claude Van Dame, Sylvester Stallion,* and

Arnold Shwazerneggar were not my personal favorites, I knew very well that they were always the 'good guys', the guys on the right side, the *American side.* I knew I had to support them in pursue of 'justice', no matter how many people they brutally killed. In the back of my mind it said; 'It is okay to kill in the name of justice'. These movie heroes, even when they were not cops in the movie in question, still had firearms and they used them. Therefore, I have always felt that it is right to own a firearm and use it, when I feel and believe it is the right thing to do. My celebrity Brother and Sister in the entertainment industry are trained and hired to portray these images and make them appealing and enticing to us, the viewers, who are, actually, law-abiding citizens. A celebrity Brother is the serial killer in the movie, portrayed as a hero. We live in a global system that plants, cultivates, and motivates criminal thinking but criminalizes a criminal act; what a contradiction, what hypocrisy. Every movie exhibits and celebrates the failure of the Black Man. Almost every movie shows fornication, one in two movies will show you adultery. A celebrity Sister in a movie is having extramarital sex, and this is perceived as heroic because her husband 'is not as sweet and romantic', or 'as good looking', or 'as kind' as the man she is having an affair with, or the Sister is simply engaging in sex before marriage; while my Brother who is a celebrity singer, sings about 'Umgwinyo' (Ecstasy), and 'Gqhe' (Vagina), and my Sister is singing "Lahl' umlenze" (Throw Your Legs Open) and singing songs about gold digging. What we give to our youth is what we give to our future. What we feed our youth today, is exactly what our youth will become tomorrow; hence *"You are what you eat."* However, do these so-called celebrities know what they are doing? Are they aware? Even comedians have become agents, making fun of one political leader while promoting another. Have they sold their souls for material wealth: fortune and fame? On the other hand, perhaps they are just ignorant kids trying to 'live big'. If only they could realize the difference between living big and living well. Making a grand example of the late singer *Whitney Houston*, leader of the *Nation of Islam, The Honorable Minister Louis Farrakhan* highlighted how the entertainment industry "promotes a decadent lifestyle that pulls our youth out of the church into the world and corrupts our youth destroying them in the process." He said:

"So you put yourself in front of the television all day looking at stupidity; put the music on 'come on baby, come on honey, shake that booty.' Is this what we teach our little girls? Is this what we see on television from the beautiful artists and entertainers? They grow up in the church then they are called out of the church to the world and the world corrupts them and spits them out."

Who wants to stay in the church and sing there? Even the so-called Gospel artists are today celebrities, and behaving like 'divas and superstars'. You find them in drug and alcohol scandals. We see them in Award shows and After Parties behaving like everybody else, meaning, drinking and talking dirty with the very same lips they proclaim to be serving and worshiping God the Almighty with through their talent. Who gave them the authority to beat on drums and blow saxes without the knowledge of the spiritual world and knowledge of Self? Was not the *unclean* musical sounds literally the work *Satan*, introduced to the people of Kane,

Brother of Abel? After *Satan's* plot worked and music became popular, was Saturday nights not reserved for music and gathering for partying? By 'Satan' I mean a deviated man whose mission was to further mislead other souls. Was this not the period when women began altering their physical and facial looks, beautifying themselves so that men would lust them? Was this not the period when people of Kane and people of the world learnt adultery and intoxication? How can the church adopt such an occult without initiation? Up until this day, Friday-Saturday, which used to be the Sabbath, a Day of Rest, is celebrated as the day to party and to 'have fun' as they called it then or *entertainment* as they call it today. Whoever told you that 'Friday-Saturday-night fun' is a culture, or urban culture, as they now call it, lied to you. This practice is not a culture, it is a ritual – a Satanic ritual, *devil worship,* a time of the week that produces many injuries and deaths.

Prophet Muhammad (pbuh) discouraged a busy lifestyle, the life lived by today's youth and adults; the up and down life, the night life, the party life. He encouraged Believers to maintain a private lifestyle. Informing his followers, he (pbuh) said: *"The one who's sitting is better than the one who's standing. The one who's standing is better than the one who's walking. The one who's walking is better than the one who's running. And if you are sitting and trouble enters your home, be like the better one of the two sons of Adam."* Shubhan'Allah.

In her memoir; *The Prisoner's Wife*, Sister *Asha Bandele* reminisces about her ignorant days as a lost youth and how her *choice* of music played a part in her chaotic lifestyle:

"Back then, songs organized all of my movements. They determined who I was friends with, what I did on weekends, everything. But as I grew older, I tried to gain control over my life, and I stopped drinking and hanging out and going to clubs, and fussing all those Friday nights into Saturdays on flashing, heated, dance floors. And when I let all of it go, I let the music go too. I did not understand how the song and the beat were

CHAPTER 9 | 156

not the problem."

Music is a bridge of communication between nations. It is through music that messages and stories are transmitted in the most practical demonstration. A nation's contemporary sound is a mirror to that nation's contemporary culture. If what I have written contains any truth, then South Afrikan artists in music, art, and film industry have no business emulating foreign artistry. We have a unique culture, a unique story, a unique message, the world is waiting on us. All that cash-flashing, ass-shaking is not who we are. Regarding my Black Brothers and Sisters, I sit and wonder, is this the Black way? I ask myself: Why are we following the ways of these Caucasians who worshipped idols and the sun and the moon and everything else besides God the Almighty? Who is it that we are trying to fool; ourselves, the people, or maybe God the Almighty Himself? Is it in any way Afrikan to get the platform to express ourselves publicly and not only dress up in a self-degrading way but also talk (sing) about what goes on privately in the Bedroom, and even more degrading, mimic the sexual act in a form of a dance? The slave master is no longer visible, no longer in the picture, and today, it is the *house nigga* who is holding the whip, doing the cracking. And who is this *house nigga* but my celebrity Brother who has taken up this position with pride sowing seeds of destruction with his words, whipping the Black youth from right to left, from morality to immorality, from Afrikan cultural values to Western secularism, from righteousness to wickedness, from light to darkness – in essence, my celebrity Brother is the new Cracker. He is the man in the spotlight with a microphone whipping Black youth to dumbness. He is not doing all this out of his will, he is taking orders from the slave master, the white man behind the curtains.

Each artist, I believe, should be a something first before being an artist. If we look at rappers, for example, who are the most influential personnel in the Black youth culture; when you ask a Rap artist what he is, he will reply, *"I am a Rapper"*, which is a wrong answer. A satisfactory answer should be *"I am a Philosopher who raps"*, or *"I am an Entertainer who raps"*, or *"Spiritual Teacher who raps"*. No one just comes 'out of the blue' and he's a Rapper. If you are a rapper and you are not dropping knowledge, you are wack,

I don't care how nice you are. RAP is *"Rhythm And Poetry"*. Rappers are poets and we all know that poets are minor prophets; they teach about the past and warn of the future. No one comes out of the blue and he's a Gospel artist; some of them are hustlers singing Gospel music, in search of riches and fame. One has to be something first. We have great artists such as *Mama Busi Mhlongo, Letta Mbuli* and *Hugh Masikela, Mawe2, Mandoza, Tuks Senganga, Molemi, Naima K*, etc, to learn from. These are story tellers and community builders. We all know very well that in our townships we do not have drug labs. Drugs are imported into our Black neighborhoods; where do they come from? None of the Rappers ever asks this question. The answer is very simple; there is a very rich white man who bribes a selfishly stupid Black government official, who allows his drugs to be smuggled into the country and distributed into our towns and neighborhoods. The more drugs they smuggle, the more money they make, the more our people become corrupted. Therefore, the more crime we have, the more broken families we have, the more prisoners we have, and, tragically, the more deaths we have.

This poor celebrity Brother is another commodity. Whenever

a big event such as *Durban July* comes along, this Brother is temporarily placed on a high pedestal, he is made to look very important at the event, and he is even labeled *VIP* (Very Important Person). The underlying purpose for all this illusionary representation is for me and you, the men down here, to buy into this meaningless event of animal abuse and gambling, to see it as something worthy, then buy entry tickets with large amounts, and bet our pennies away – while none of us asks the question of where is all this money going. Who are the organizers? What are we to profit – to gain, or are we just meant to spend – or to lose? Black people dominate every social event like a rally, even the poorest of the poor get consumed by such events, even though, always, they are spat out like saliva the moment the event is over, and the organizers are packing their luggage and passports getting ready for an overseas holiday trip, while you and I are back in the ghetto, again, struggling to get bread, and struggling to keep the lights on and water running. This is definitely not to say we should not attend such shows if we feel we are going to enjoy ourselves. But this is to say we must get our priorities straight – do we want to dance with chains or do we want to be free? A temporary happiness is an illusion of joy. I choose freedom, the choice is yours too. If you stress about going to a *Lil 'Wayne* concert, and yet you cannot afford yourself a decent bed to sleep in, you are not free, you are what I call a *Modern-Day Slave*, you are still in chains, mental chains.

The Messenger of Islam (pbuh) had a simple, strong, and beautiful prayer, he said: *"O Allah, show me things as they are, so I might not be deceived by how they appear to be."*

It was revealed in the holy Book that on the Day of Judgement, those who went astray would cry out to Satan, shouting; *"…but you promised us; you promised us the promise of Truth"*, and he will say unto them; *"I had no authority over you, but I called you, and you came."* And these are their own desires. This is falsehood; the television, the media, it is all a big Lie, it's an invitation to blindness, an invitation to hell on earth, you can accept it or decline it, you have a choice. May Almighty God make from us those who make the right choices.

CHAPTER 10

In Conclusion: A solution by a Blackman

A Blackman is a Conditioned man.

In our evaluation and examination of the plight and condition of the Black man caused by many different historical and present events, social and political strife, we shall now try to find a solution to all our problems, those which made us seem to the world – and tragically, to ourselves – as problematic. This solution has to be one but multi-dimensional, flexible yet fundamental and radical. A common ground for all ethnic, religious, and political groups must be found by all means. Not surprisingly, it is impossible to talk about *any* kind of solution without using Godly ways as a primary blueprint; we are religious people by nature dealing with a divine cause called *unity*. However, the idea or concept of so-called God and so-called God's Command is different for different religious groups, cultures, and individuals. Again, we will look at this *Solution* using South Afrika as our point of geographical reference. We will touch on South Afrikan politics, religion, traditions and cultures. In order to get straight to the solution quicker, I will be very frank, at times brutally frank. This Chapter is merely an attempt. Therefore, anyone and everyone is welcome to argue, challenge and debate anything we will discuss; in that case we will learn from each other. What we first need to understand and agree on is the fact that we will never get anything right until we get the right idea and knowledge of who God The Almighty, the Creator of heaven and earth, is. I assume we all agree that there is *a* God, the Creator of Heaven and Earth, and that He exists. That being said, we can now move forth, but first, let us look back in retrospect remembering our original Afrikan traditional belief; did we, as Black people of South Afrika ever believe in many gods? No. We believed in One Supreme God, who we called uMvelinqangi: "Mveli" meaning *Lo Owavela* (the One Who Appeared), and "Nqangi" meaning "Unknown". We know Him also as "Lo Owavela Kuqala" (the One Who

Appeared First). We do not know where He came from but we do know that He created Himself and all that exists. In Afrikan mythology, He was not born and He did not beget. He has no gender. He had no parents, nor did He have any friends. The Christian idea of Jesus being the son of God, in a literal sense, is foreign to the Black South Afrikan and Afrikan in general.

The problems of men are caused by either religion or lack of religion. People who do not follow any religion are convinced that their lives are greater because they are free from rules and dogma imposed upon so-called religious individuals. They believe themselves to be free from anything, they can do whatever they see suitable, and they can worship God in their own way without being told by anyone or any Book how to, and when to. In all this, they depend solely on their intuition and conscience as their moral guide, or perhaps, reading spiritual books written by men of intellect but ultimately men like them, or attending spiritual classes tutored by qualified professors and spiritual gurus and men of great wisdom. Most of them do believe in God but because they have been let down by religions they were once part of, or because they have been discouraged by all that they observe daily from so-called religious individuals and groups, they ultimately made a conscious decision to stay not only religionless but also anti-religion, although still religious in some form. It seems to me as though they believed in men more than they believed in God – the same as people who say they cannot become Muslims because of how terribly Muslims (Indians, Malaysians, and Afghanistanis) treat Black people who work for them, and those who say they cannot become Christians because of the way Black people have been exploited, enslaved, and colonized for decades by the so-called Christian world and emperors. These individuals are not guided by cultural values, though they believe in some of them, and they are not guided by religious values either, but rather 'moral values' even though they quote from Scriptures now and again. Their culture is different from religious and traditional cultures. In both tradition and religion, there is what we can justly call dogma. If a tradition does not permit women to wear pants, the traditional woman must try to look for and find logic in this objection. If a religion discourages gambling, the religious man in question must also look for and find reasonable grounds in this discouragement. There is no room for arguments and objections – you cannot testify against this, you can only rebel. Since unguided morality has no basis other than conscience, which is no dogma, the moral principles are bound to change from time to time. And, needless to say, in many ways, they are guaranteed to fail you – and they have. If you are one of these people, it will be untrue for you to say in your life you didn't make any mistakes – yes you wouldn't want to change them because they taught you a lesson or two, however, sooner or later, one mistake will leave you with no lesson to learn from for it will be a fatal one. If we look at the suicide rate, for instance, this group has the largest number of depressions and suicides compared to religiously and traditionally cultured youth whose lives are rooted in faith before solutions. Even more so, 'Morality Rule' is an individualistic approach, therefore is bound to result in a conflict of interests between individuals within the community. It will not get us anywhere as a unit, a society – it is the opposite of *socialism*. Self-independence is an illusion; it is a Western concept which sugarcoats selfishness and greed. In Afrika we always had societies of families with traditions, never were we without one. Therefore, we shall shelve this ideology for it does not serve a communal purpose.

Moving on – *Tradition?* Could it be the answer to the Black man's plight? Well, there are a few things to say about tradition. Firstly, it has been tried and tested, and just like Christianity, it failed its believers and practitioners. The reasons for this failure could be many, or perhaps just one. The reason for this failure could be because it was not *followed accordingly*, or maybe that it did not provide enough theoretical, even worse, practical evidence and solution to all of the people's problems; and personally I refuse to accept the latter. As we all know, for a tradition to be followed accordingly, one must be thoroughly informed on the subject at hand, for it is the traditional laws which makes a people's culture smooth and enjoyable, so where did we go wrong? Undoubtedly, a major reason for our cultural downfall is the clash between traditional culture and the European Christian culture. As *Steve Biko* puts it in his book, *"I Write What I Like"*:

The two major cultures that met and 'fused' were

the African Culture and the Anglo-Boer culture. Whereas the African culture was unsophisticated and simple, the Anglo-Boer culture had all the trappings of a colonialist culture and therefore was heavily equipped for conquest. Where they could, they conquered by persuasion, using a highly exclusive religion that denounced all other Gods and demanded a strict code of behavior with respect to clothing, education ritual and custom. Where it was impossible to convert, firearms were readily available and used to advantage. Hence, the Anglo-Boer culture was the more powerful culture in almost all facets. This is where the African began to lose a grip on himself and his surroundings."

Now that we are clear, we can begin our scrutiny of *Tradition*. In our discussion, we will use historical references and records such as History books and Religious scriptures, especially the Holy Bible and the Glorious Koran. The reason for usage of religious scriptures is that they are the most credible scriptures containing a vast ancient history of men and their not-so-ancient evolution and the most compact story of God, the Creator. In most cases, Religion and the Afrikan Tradition will oppose, but where they are not opposing, it will be with the Koran, not the Bible, and this proves something very significant, which will reveal itself along the way. Tragically, the one point of conflict between the Koran and *modern* Tradition, but where the Bible and *modern* Tradition agree, is crucial. This is the fact that in a time of need, in desperate moments, as modern traditionalists we cry out to the dead, and go to Izangoma (practitioners of magic, fortune/future tellers) for help. In the Islamic world this is unforgiveable.

In their call to the dead and practices of animal sacrifice to human deities, uMvelinqangi says in the holy *Koran 6:136:*

> "They set aside for God a share in what He (uMvelinqangi) has produced, such as crops and livestock, and they say, 'this is for God' – so they claim! – and 'this is for our associate-gods? Their associate-gods' share does not

> reach God, whereas God's share reaches their
> associates-gods. How ill they judge!"

Allah calls this practice an invention, and needless to say, it is forbidden, while on the other hand Christians call out to Jesus and bow down under statues of Jesus, Mary, and all the other biblical Saints. It must be said that both groups, the modern traditionalist and the Christian, as much as they claim the dead and Jesus are no more than intermediaries whose task is to pass the message to God, by the look of things through close examination, we cannot shake off the feeling, or ignore the observance, that this practice has been taken out of context, and these so-called intermediaries have become deities themselves, and have ultimately replaced God, the Almighty, or at least, have been elevated to His level. Does our Bible, in *Exodus 20* not say; *Do not worship any other gods besides me*? In most cases, during a Christian prayer and modern Traditionalist talk, God will either be sidelined, or completely absent, while the name "Jesus" and names of the dead are proclaimed over and over again. Islamically, this is the ultimate blasphemy. Allah says in the Glorious

Koran 39:3 *"It is to God alone that sincere obedience is due. And those who take other guardians besides Him say, 'We serve them only that they may bring us nearer to God'"*. The verse continues: *"God does not guide anyone who is bent on lying and is a disbelieving lair"*. In 46:4 (Koran): *"Say, 'Have you thought about those you call upon apart from God? Show me what they have created on the earth. Or do they have a share in the heavens? Bring me a Book revealed before this or some other vestige of knowledge, if you are telling the truth."* In Islam God is our *only* help and He has no helper or intermediary.

Islam and Christianity share a lot of beliefs and practices. Muslims also believe in Angels, the Judgment Day, and obviously God, Who in Arabic is referred to as Allah. Christians also believe in Fasting and Prayer. However, in our tradition we do not believe that uMvelinqangi has any children, or a son, neither does a Muslim believe such claims. On the other hand Islam teaches that Allah (Mvelinqangi) since the beginning of time has sent down about 124 000 Prophets. *"According to the Islamic tradition, prophets are given to all people. Luqman, an Afrikan, was one of the wisest prophets who has an entire Chapter (in the Holy Koran) dedicated to him. But unlike some other Prophets who only came for a localized area, Muhammad is a prophet/messenger for humanity".* All these Prophets were sent to confirm teachings of previous Messengers and teach men about God, and they were sent into every nation. The Koran says: *"We have sent in every nation a messenger so you would know the power of Allah."* Their assignment was to lead men back to the right path when they have de-railed from the Path of God. Here in South Afrika, for instance, we always knew God the All Mighty, we called Him uMvelinqangi, and this we knew before the white man touched our soil, meaning, we too had a messenger or messengers who told us about God. They may not have carried any scriptures but they carried the same message as in the scriptures.

The Koran (Wisdom) answers questions anyone might have about the ancient time, in the modern world, and about the future in this world and the Hereafter – *"We have put forth for men in this Koran every kind of parable in order that they may receive admonition"* 39:27. There is a solution to gambling, intoxication, racism, child breeding, women abuse, money, false politics and politicians, 'entertainment', to name the least. Another important verse regarding this, is

18:54: "We have explained in detail in this Koran for the benefit of mankind every kind of similitude: but man is, in most things, contentious (argumentative without knowledge)." It should be noted that the Wisdom of Allah cannot be contained in any physical Book or Books. Holy Scriptures are very important revelations for warning and awareness, and wisdom is within you and in all of creation around you. *Prophet Muhammad* (pbuh) said, *"Travel the whole world in search for knowledge".* He could have said, *"Read a Book".*

We don't believe in a God that is looking and talking to us from the sky. We believe in a God that is within us and within all creation, we look at one another and see Him, honor Him, and know Him.

Comments from non-Muslim scholars and observers regarding the Final Messenger (pbuh) includes *Prof. K. S. Ramakrishna rao,* and he says of the Prophet of Allah (pbuh):

> "The personality of Muhammad, it is most difficult to get into the whole truth of it. Only a glimpse of it I can catch. What a dramatic

succession of picturesque? There is Muhammad, the Prophet. There is Muhammad, the General; Muhammad, the King; Muhammad, the Preacher; Muhammad, the Philosopher; Muhammad, the Statesman; Muhammad, the Orator; Muhammad, the Reformer; Muhammad, the Refuge of Orphans; Muhammad, the Protector of Slaves; Muhammad, the Emancipator of Women; Muhammad, the Judge; Muhammad, the Saint. And in all these magnificent roles, in all these departments of human activities, he is like a hero."

Alphonse Lamartine, French poet, said of the Prophet of God (pbuh): *"Philosopher, Orator, Apostle, Legislator, Warrior, Conqueror of ideas, the Restorer of rational beliefs, the Preacher of a religion without images, the Founder of twenty terrestrials empires and of one heavenly Empire, that is Muhammad. As regards all standards (I repeat 'ALL') by which human greatness may be measured, we may well ask, is there any man greater than he?"*

An average South Afrikan citizen, regardless of race and age, needs to get familiar with this noble character; research him, study him. As for the Black mother, and Black father, do more research, go beyond, learn further, for your Black child is in darkness looking for answers to Life, and when she finds Islam, she will embrace it. Therefore, brace yourself, for if you fight it you will lose her, because she would rather lose you than lose Islam; do not make the mistake of making her choose. Another un-biased scholar, amongst many, *Jules Masserman*, U. S. Psychoanalyst, says in *Time* magazine of July 15 1974:

"Leaders must fulfill three functions:

1. Provide for the wellbeing of the led,

2. Provide a social organization in which people feel relatively secure, and

3. Provide them with one set of beliefs.

People like Pasteur and Salk are leaders in the first sense.

> People like Gandhi and Confucius, on one hand, and Alexander, Caesar and Hitler on the other hand, are leaders in the second and perhaps the third sense. Jesus and Buddha belong to the third category alone.

PERHAPS THE GREATEST LEADER OF ALL TIMES WAS MOHAMMAD, WHO COMBINED ALL THREE FUNCTIONS."

I will put more emphasis on and references from the holy Koran for one reason; in this country, it is no household scripture as compared to the holy Bible and Traditional customs.

Again, to make things easier we will only discuss the issues which these three 'solution contenders' disagree upon, not where they all agree. And we will not dwell on universally accepted solutions such as issues of raising children. Our Afrikan Tradition and Islam agree that there is only One God and God is One. Christianity says He is Three in One or

One in Three (Holy Trinity). Christians are to pray 'in the name of Jesus', and we shout, "*Jesus is Lord*", he is "*King of kings*", "*Lord of lords*". In Islam this claim is frowned upon. These are attributions to God, and God only. The Glorious Koran talks to every tribesman, caveman, indigenous man, warning us sternly against this claim and reminding us that this claim is actually foreign to all mankind. "*(And to warn) those who say, 'God has taken to Himself a son.' They have no knowledge of this, nor did their forefathers have any either. What they say is monstrous: they are merely uttering falsehood!*" In Islam, praying in the name of Prophet Muhammad (pbuh) or any other person or Prophet is blasphemy, Islam teaches us: "*There is none worthy of worship besides Allah. He is alone. He has no partner. To Him alone does everything belong and He alone deserves all praise and He has power over everything.*" The Prophet (pbuh) forbade Muslims from praising him in a manner that would lead to people worshiping him: "*Do not exaggerate in praising me as the Christians praised the son of Mary, for I am only a slave. So, call me the slave of Allah and His apostle.*" This fault, however, cannot be placed upon our beloved Prophet Jesus (pbuh) because he never once claimed to be God the Almighty, or even claimed any kind of divinity, he even refused being called "Good" or "Righteous". In the Bible, in *St Mark 10:17-18* it is written: *"As he was starting out on a trip, a man came running up to Jesus, knelt down, and asked: 'Good Teacher, what should I do to get eternal life?' 'Why do you call me good?' Jesus asked, Only God is truly good'"*.

In his book *Ubhaqa*, *Sheikh Dawood Ngwane*, late Veteran Attorney who abandoned his high position in church and accepted the teachings of Islam, writes: *"Jesus (PBUH) had many opportunities to explain who he was. If he was a part of a Trinity God he would have said so. Just think carefully!"* This is another absolute lie invented by the enemies of God, Jesus (PBUH) never said such a thing, in *5:116* of the *Koran*, it says:

"When God says, 'Jesus, son of Mary, did you say to people, "Take me and my mother as two deities besides God"? He will answer, 'Glory be to You! How could I ever say that to which I have no right? If I ever said so, You would surely have known it. You know what is in my mind, while I do not know anything that is within Yours. You alone are the Knower of unseen things – I told them only what You commanded me to, "Worship God, my Lord and your Lord."

In *5:17*, the Holy *Koran* reads; *"In blasphemy indeed are those who say 'God is Christ, the son of Mary.' Say, 'Who then could prevent God if He so willed from destroying Christ, son of Mary, and his mother and everyone on earth? The kingdom of the heavens and the earth and everything between them belong to God. He creates what He will and God has power over all things.'*

Unlike Christianity, Judaism can remove the Prophet Moses (pbuh) and there will still be Jews; in Islam, the Prophet Muhammad (pbuh) can be removed from the religion and yet we will still have Islam and we will still have Muslims. As for Christianity, we remove Jesus (pbuh) and we have no Christianity and we have no Christians. This should tell us something very important and very clear – Islam is the religion of/about/from God and Christianity is a religion of/about Christ (as the name suggests), but not from Christ. Therefore, Christians worship a man and Muslims and Jews worship God. Conservative Christians say: "God is

Almighty, therefore He can become whatever He wants to become, NOTHING is impossible with Him", and I say; "Yes He is". We agree, and in our agreement we ask; "Can you as a human being become a doctor or schoolteacher, or president of the country, if you aspire to?" And the conservative Christian says "Yes, and we can become lawyers, surfers, boxers, nurses, etc." And then we ask; "Can you as a human being become a dog, or a lion, or a brick, or a glass, or a cell phone?" And they say "No, that is impossible". And again we agree. In this, we draw a lesson that a human being can become *anything* he desires, as long as that which he desires is human, and yes, God can become anything He desires without an effort but that which God desires also must be Godly. And remember that being God is being Supreme over all things, it is Ultimate Perfection. Let us explain further: In Islam, uMvelinqangi is a Supreme Being, the All-Creator, who does not become a man, for man is limited and God is not; and that is what makes Him 'God' in the first place.

"Man by nature eats, sleeps and answers the call of nature. Hence, all of these form part of man's daily necessities. Man is dependent on sleep in order to refresh himself. If he didn't sleep, he would be terribly exhausted and not be able to work. Likewise, a man is DEPENDENT on food to gain energy, if he didn't eat, he would die of hunger. Therefore, God Almighty would not adopt an attribute which reflects dependency; because God is INDEPENDENT." – *Islaminfo* Magazine. And again: God does not depend on anything yet everything (tangible and intangible, living or dead) depends on him.

"None can be one with God physically, because He is not a physical Being." – Sheikh Ahmed Deedat.

In the book *Ubhaqa, Sheikh Dawood Ngwane* reveals a despicable statement by his former priest. He writes: **"Before I embraced Islam in 1996 I visited a Roman Catholic priest, Reverend Father Doncabe, who had offered to assist me understand Christianity in order to stop me from embracing Islam. I found the priest seated behind a huge desk with three Bibles opened in different places. He stood up as I entered and came forward to shake my hand. As he held my hand he said:** *"Mr NGWANE,* *before we begin our talk we must agree on something."* **I asked, still holding his hand,** *"and what is that?"* **He said** *"that we as Christians believe in the Bible as the word of God and we also believe in the Doctrine of the Church".*

I was puzzled because I thought the Doctrine of the Church would be based on the Bible. I did not know what the doctrine of the church was something apart from the Bible and I asked: *"Is the doctrine of the church different from what is in the Bible?"* *"Yes",* **confessed the priest.** *"There are matters which are not in the Bible which we believe in because the church tells us to believe in, which are the doctrine of the church".* *"Like what for example?"* **I prodded.** *"Like the doctrine of the Trinity"* **said the priest.** *"This doctrine you cannot find anywhere in the Bible but we believe in it because it is the doctrine of the church"*

I was actually shocked to hear this; I began to think of the millions of people, clever people all over the world, doctors in the various academic professions, professors, lawyers and academics who are clinging onto something that does not exist. The priest could see the shock on my face and he emphasized *"you can read your Bible from the first to the last page and you will not find that God is a Trinity".* *"Then* *where do you get it from?"* **I asked**. *"As I told you, it is the Doctrine of the Church"* responded the priest. *"Where does the Church get it from?"* **I insisted**. *"We do not ask where the Church gets its doctrine from; as Christians we believe in what the Church teaches without asking such questions."* **I actually said** *"but that is stupid"*. **These words escaped from my lips and I quickly checked myself and without apologizing said:** *"Well you have admitted defeat before we have even started because I have come to argue that God is not a Trinity. If your doctrine has no basis how can you convince me that God is a Trinity?"* **I do not believe that any priest or Bishop could have done better than Father Doncabe, for no priest or Bishop will be able to show where in the Bible Jesus (PBUH) said that God is a trinity and that he himself was part of that Trinity. The best any priest or Bishop will do is quote from Paul, who is called 'the apostle'; for it is Paul who is the architect of present day Christianity (a former avowed enemy of the Christians) and is therefore their source of reference."**

If you align nothing along with God and place no one between you and Him, you feel even closer to Him, therefore developing more love for Him. Moses (pbuh) did not preach Judaism, Jesus (pbuh) never preached Christianity; every single prophet of Allah preached *The Laws of God* in short: *Islam*.

Islamically, Tradition and Religion cannot be separated and made into two opposing components, for they do not oppose each other. In a book called *AFRICANA*, on *Islam and Tradition*, writer *Lamine Sanneh* gives five points on the topic:

> The Prophet enjoys a special status (wahy) as God's approved messenger.
>
> The Prophet's sunnah (tradition), therefore, has lying upon it the seal of divine approval.
> The sunnah of the Prophet and the Koran as the book of revelation, are always in agreement.
>
> Therefore, conflict between the sunnah and the Koran cannot happen.
>
> The sunnah can replace the Koran if the Koran has nothing to say on any subject. But even if

the Koran has something to say, the sunnah
can still provide complementary explanations.

On issues of *Adultery* our Tradition is not very vocal but one
of the accepted rules is that we are to punish our wives by
hitting them very lightly when being disrespectful. We, as
husbands, are to hit them very lightly with the palm
anywhere below the neck. If the husband in question
disregards this rule, he is to be hit by his wife's brothers (but
after the matter has been presented to the committee of
elders in the village). The same chapter (*Deuteronomy 25:11-
12*) that talks about womens' hand being cut off, also talks
about stoning. *Deuteronomy 22 verse 22-24, Lev. 20:10* and
Proverbs 6:20 & 7:27 say that both the adulterers must be
stoned to death, while the Koran 24:2 says *Flog the adulteress
and the adulterer, each of them, with a hundred lashes.* In the
same Chapter, *verse four* it says (in protection of women from
being falsely accused): *Those who defame chaste women, but
cannot produce four (eye) witnesses, shall be given eighty lashes.
Do not accept their testimony ever after, for they are transgressors,
save those who afterwards repent and make amends, for truly God
is forgiving and merciful.*

The issue of *Drugs and Alcohol*: in our Tradition we have what we call *IsiZulu*, which is home-brewed traditional beer, and because of this innovation, drinking has become easily acceptable among men and husbands. It is an innovation. The title "UmZulu" simply means "Ocwebileyo" (The Pure One). Needless to say, the 'pure one' can't be in a state of drunkenness, it has never been part of our culture to drink alcohol.

According to the Bible, Jesus turned water into wine as his first miracle, and in some churches, they ritually drink the wine representing 'Jesus' blood', moreover, in *1 Timothy 5;23* it says: *"Don't drink only water. You ought to drink a little wine for the sake of your stomach because you are sick so often."* Again, perhaps this is why some Christians assume it is okay to drink wine outside church, when out 'wining and dining'. The holy Koran says *Gambling and intoxication is the abomination from the work of Satan.* In Islam, alcoholic wine is haraam (forbidden).

On *Marriage:* first and foremost, in Islam extremism is not allowed, Islam teaches a balanced lifestyle; not too much materialism and not too much spiritualism to the extent that a person takes the Catholic stance as to avoid anything worldly and humanly such as sex and marriage. However, generally all three cultures encourage marriage. They all agree that sex before marriage is forbidden. However, there are areas where they differ, for example: the Tradition obliges *Ilobolo* before marriage, Christianity forbids polygamy, and in Islam, polygamy is acceptable but optional and *ilobolo* is required, in its original pattern. *Dr. Reggie Khumalo*, Traditionalist, writer and Philosopher shares his deep knowledge on the history of *Ilobolo*:

> "Originally, the grooms' family would give gifts to the brides' parents as a symbol of gratitude for raising a young girl to a woman. Then things changed to cows only: one for the brides' mother, one for the father, and the last cow for a farewell 'celebration'.
>
> Then, when the white people (Christian missionaries) arrived here in South Africa, their mission was to put an end to polygamy,

and they achieved it through *Sir Shepstone* –
now the number of cows went up to eleven,
which is also the number that is still used for
ilobolo until this day."

This being said, it is quite clear that *ilobolo* as we know it
today was never a true traditional practice, it is nothing less
than a fabrication and fraud by an illegal immigrant colonist
invader named *Theophelus Shepstone*. The groom's giving of
the gifts or three cows was very significant, yes, but it was
merely a 'Thank You' gesture, and the acceptance of these
gifts or three cows was a 'handshake' of peace and joining
between the two families. Christian missionaries on the
other hand succeeded in their mission of ending polygamy
in the Black culture and caused harm, which is irreversible,
putting Black people into marital debts which caused most
to remain unmarried, therefore lacking strong family
structure, which is a foundation of good upbringing and the
basis for blessings. Unless and until we adopt the Islamic
way of marriage where only witnesses and immediate
family can be your guests, and a cash gift to your bride of as

low as a R100 and as high as R1000, or go back to the traditional way of Gifts or three cows, which is reasonable, and which I doubt would be accepted in this day and age because the once traditional humble Black man and woman are arrogant and boastful of their new westernized selves, the selves that they are not. We have to understand and realize the differences between a way made by God and one made by men (inspired by Satan). When God lays down a guideline He makes it easily reachable and timeless. He cannot tell us to do something and then make it hard for us to. He ordered us to worship Him, and made it easy. He ordered us to marry each other, and again made it easy to get married – requirements: groom, bride, two witnesses (one for each), a marriage officer, and we have a new family. Ways of men are always hard, short lived, and their test is always monetary. God ways requires patience and faith.

Black Christians who can afford to wed (actually who can afford big bank loans) usually practice what they call 'white wedding'. Only recently have they combined both 'traditional wedding' and 'white' or 'Western' wedding. However, truthfully speaking, the so-called traditional wedding is nothing more than traditional outfits and hymns.

They merely waste their money on a so-called traditional wedding, which is completely separate from an indigenous marriage, which permits polygamy and disfavors divorce. We forget that a wedding is something for the day, but a marriage stays with the couple for as long as they live.

In the Hadith it states: *"Be kind towards your women. Take heed! You have rights over your women and your women also have rights over you. Their rights over you are that you provide food and clothing for them in good faith. Your rights over them are that they do not allow and nor do they give permission, for people to trespass into your house whose presence you dislike."*

Still on Marriage and protection of women in Islam, the religion known to many for being 'abusive' and 'hostile' towards women: one would find it rather strange or even shocking to learn that in Islam there is no such thing as 'Husband and Wife', as they say in the so-called Modern Society, but rather, in Allah's Governance, the pair is labeled 'Companions'. This is the symbol of equality. Moreover, Muslim women, by common law, are not to change their last names after marriage. The reason for this is that Islam recognizes each individual as that – an individual, an independent human being; a human being whose rights cannot be stripped no matter what the condition, a human being who has every right to know their linage. In Islam if a man is not your biological father you are not to take and use his surname. As for the married woman, being married does not mean you are no longer your father's child, therefore taking up a new surname breaks the chain of linage and creates a false personality, which is a personality built by façade upon façade. Some of you may understand this very well, and some may say this is foolishness. Now let us look back into our Afrikan tradition; what do you call a newly married woman from the *Dlamini* tribe? Do not be mistaken, in our tradition and language we do not have the title 'Mrs.' This new bride in our culture is now referred to as *'maDlamini'* not *Mrs Mthethwa*, because it is her husband who is born from the Mthethwa tribe not her. *King Shaka's* mother was known as *Nandi ka Bhebhe*. Even though she was married to *Senzangakhona ka Jama* as his third wife, she was never called "Nandi ka Jama" because *Bhebhe* was her father not *Jama*. Let me remind you my beloved Brothers and

Sisters this book is not a call to Islam, it's a call *back* to Islam, which truly is what we call IsiNtu. Some would say that women in Islam are spoilt rotten, but the truth is that women have been too oppressed for too long under the banners of 'Modernism', 'Civilization', 'Democracy', 'Liberation', and even 'Feminism', that these basic rights seem like luxurious privileges. Despite some bad deeds of some misguided Muslim men, women in Islam are nevertheless placed on a most high status and are more protected compared to any civilization you can think of. And the proof of this claim is testified in the very Words of the Koran in which Women have an entire Surah (Chapter) dedicated to them, *Al Nisa* (The Women). Still on matters of marriage; In one Hadith, the Prophet (pbuh) says: *"The greatest sin amongst all sins in the eyes of Allah, is of a person who marries a woman and divorces her once his needs have been fulfilled and also usurps her dowry in the process."* Men are also protected: *"The fragrance of Jannah (Paradise) is unlawful upon that woman who asks her husband for divorce for no apparent reason."*

Surely, in Islam, women are allowed to ask for divorce,

moreover, they are also allowed to propose to men for marriage. And in Islam, a proposal is only for marriage. This is the religion that gave women a right to divorce before any so-called civilized nation, no wonder that a legion of former feminists found solace in Islam. In this beautiful country, amongst the Black people, marriage is one of our fundamental issues that needs to be addressed, debated if it has to, and resolved immediately. It is an issue of urgency, it is a life and death issue, our survival as a nation depends on it. Without marriage we have no families, and without the family we have no homes, therefore no basis for a stable life. When I say 'we', I am talking about the child, the man and the woman in the Black community. The Prophet (pbuh) said: "Marriage is the basis for blessings." The Bible and Torah have beautiful words on marriage as well, so does our Tradition. We need more married women, there are very few married. But what we need more are women who want to marry, the 'want' should be in her actions, in her tongue, in her voice, in her talk, in her walk, in the way she dresses her body, if she dresses at all. There are more women than men, that is what population statistics tell us. South Afrika is no exception to this phenomenon, therefore, constructive polygamy proves to be culturally vital in our near future if we want to progress, and if we want to progress now.

The holy *Koran 4:3* states clearly that *Polygamy* is encouraged, advisable, but optional and subjective: *"If you fear that you shall not be able to deal justly with the orphans, marry women of your choice, twos, threes, or fours; but if you fear that you might not be able to treat them with equal fairness, then marry only one."* Clearly, in Islam polygamy is first option. In his book *Women in Islam, Dr. Sherif Abdel Azeem* writes: *"the issue of polygamy in Islam cannot be understood apart from community obligations towards orphans and widows. Islam as a universal religion suitable for all places and all times could not ignore these compelling obligations."*

Without ignoring the fact that women outnumber men four to one, polygamy seems to be a fair solution to this problem. Sheikh *Dawood Ngwane*, author of *Ubhaqa* writes:

"It is natural that a woman will want to get married. This desire is in every young woman's heart. She silently plans her contemplated future home and waits for a proposal to come her way. For some the proposal will come at an early age and for others at a later stage and yet for others it never comes." He concludes: "Nowadays the problem is much more serious as the law now permits men to find solace in other men, thus adding to the number of women who cannot find a husband." He adds: "WHAT HAPPENS TO THE SURPLUS WOMEN? Nature has it that a woman who has reached the age of adulthood will want to have a man for companionship and solace. The men who are already married to *"one wife"* will be the companions of these unfortunate ones who have not found themselves single partners: this is the Western Civilization's way of life. It is not something that is spoken about openly. Women get into this kind of relationship knowing that the man is already married but hoping that the man will divorce his wife and marry them. Sooner or later, the woman will be nursing a baby … and the next." He asks: "WHERE WILL THIS END? They are given funny names because they cannot share the title of "*wife*": they are called "mistresses / concubines / studs". He continues: "Islam says DO NOT ABUSE THEM, MARRY THEM. Let them share the title of wife. First, second, third or fourth, so that you are held responsible for their maintenance and the maintenance of all your children, not some of your children. THIS IS A SOUND SOLUTION."

In matters of *Racism* and Islam: well, since I am the only Muslim in the department I work in currently, I am usually approached by a few of my colleagues to confirm rumors they hear/heard about Islam. The most fascinating yet outrageous rumor I was recently asked to confirm was: *"Is it true that the Koran says that a dog is better than a black person and that black people are not allowed inside the mosque therefore they worship from outside?"* I could not believe that there are people who invent such statements. Allah, in the holy Koran states: *"And mankind is nothing but a single nation."* If we are a single nation, there is no room for racism and discrimination. In a letter *Malcolm X* wrote to his people from Mecca after a highlight experience of his life, he stated:

> "America needs to understand Islam, because this is the one religion that erases from its society the race problem. Throughout my travels in the Muslim world, I have met, talked to, and even eaten with people who in America would have been considered white, but the white attitude was removed from their minds by the religion of Islam. I have never before seen sincere and true brotherhood practiced by all together, irrespective of colour."

On *Democracy*, the great Hindu poetess, *Sirojini "Nightingale of India" Naidu* said of Islam: *"It was the first religion that preached and practiced democracy; for, in the mosque when the call from the Minaret is sounded and the worshippers are gathered together, the democracy of Islam is embodied five times a day when the peasant and the king kneel side by side and proclaim, "Allahu*

Akbar" (God alone is great) I have been struck over and over again by this indivisible unity of Islam that makes a man distinctively a brother."

Our traditional religion condones communion, Islam encourages Brotherhood, and Christianity promotes unity. All praises due to the Most High. The Koran teaches us that uMvelinqangi created Man from black clay, in *6:2* and *15:26*. Islam goes on to teach us that Adam (pbuh) was the prophet of Allah, and he taught 'Islam' (IsiNtu) to his children. Originally, the name Adam itself means 'Dark' or 'Dark-skinned'. He (Adam) preached Islam, so do all thousands of other prophets and messengers after him. Islam was once again revealed for the final time to the messenger, prophet, and reformer named *Ahmad* (meaning the Trustworthy), whose birth name was *Muhammad Bin Abdullah,* this time revealed as a complete and compact Divine Governance, whereas for the people of the Black continent it was and always will be his natural way of life called IsiNtu.

"Regarding some of the comments about Islam

recognizing Judaism and Christianity, I would like to clarify one thing. Islam says that both Moses and Jesus Christ were very important prophets of Allah. They brought forth true books – the Torah and Injeel (Gospels) and the name of their religion was actually Islam. Moses did not preach 'Judaism' and Jesus did not preach 'Christianity'. These terms were coined after them. Also, the rules preached by Jesus superseded those of Moses so that in the time of Jesus if somebody ONLY followed Moses' teachings he would be committing a sin. Similarly, the teachings of Prophet Muhammad (pbuh) have superseded those of Moses and Jesus. Furthermore, the Jews and Christians have made changes to their holy books so that in this point in time we cannot say which parts of the Bible or Torah are valid and which ones have been changed." Writes one blogger.

Regarding Islam being a so-called new phenomenon to Black Americans and other Black people in foreign lands, one source says, *"Among slaves, Islam in America was forbidden because owners feared it could influence rebellion. By the mid Nineteenth Century most slaves had lost understanding of their ORIGINAL faith and converted to Christianity. Not until more than two generations after the Emancipation Proclamation would Islam AGAIN surface among African Americans. And when it did it was often more of a call to RACIAL PRIDE and NATIONALISM than a call to prayer."*

Doctors, Imams, Teachers, Scientists, Mathematicians, Astrologers, were taken from Afrika as Muslims, brought to America and made into slaves. Therefore, this was no conversion; to convert is to drop something for another, as we dropped Islam for Christianity, which made us Christian converts. However, when one goes back to his original faith or belief, it is called reverting; it is to revert, which makes us Muslim reverts – those of us who have been Christian converts.

"It Is He Who named you Muslims, both before and in this (REVELATION); that the Apostle may be a witness for you, and you may be witnesses for mankind." – *Koran 22:78.*

Another credible source says; *"Although Islam is regarded as the youngest of all revealed religions, it is NOT A NEW RELIGION, but a continuation of the first religion of God to Man, purged and purified, time after time, from all human adulterations and restored to its original purity."* – *Muslims at Prayer,* brochure published by *IPCI* (Islamic Propagation Centre International).

Allah says in the holy *Koran,* 5:3; *This day I have perfected for you your Divine Governance and completed My favor upon you and have approved for you Islam as Governance.* Islam is therefore a favor and an Order from Allah. It is a complete favor, there is no other favor regarding Governance except Islam.

Islam on *Revolution, Oppression and Political Involvement*: the Glorious *Koran* makes it clear that it is a sin not only to oppress others but even to oppress yourself or to allow oppression upon yourself. ICSA (Islamic Council of South Africa), in May 1981, condemned the 20th anniversary of the Republic celebration and appealed to Muslims not to participate therein. In 1983 ICSA also rejected the Government's proposal for a new Constitution and the President's Council because Blacks in the country were excluded from participating, saying that *"as Muslims we resent being labeled 'Indian', 'Coloured', 'Malay', 'Bantu', or 'White'"*. Furthermore, former President *Nelson Mandela* at the *Oxford Centre for Islamic Studies*, 11 July 1997 said: *"I would like to take this opportunity to pay tribute to South African Muslims who died while in detention because of their resistance to apartheid; Babla Saloojee; Imam Haron; Ahmed Timol; and Dr Hussein Haffejee. They represent the involvement of the Muslim community in the struggle for justice and freedom, also does the presence of Muslims as cabinet Ministers and in the highest office of our judiciary, in the new democratic political dispensation of our country."*

The Muslim involvement is underrated and unknown, and mostly overlooked by those political figures who know it. This mistake needs to be corrected, and only Muslims themselves have to correct it. One blogger replying to accusations of Black Muslims being misguided and of Islam not being a true and original religion for the Black man, wrote: *"Even if Islam were false you would be politically idiotic and dogmatic to waste time on converting them. Black Muslims are devout Pan-Afrikanists with a revolutionary history and character, all that you are doing is delaying the movement by creating internal strife. You have provided no evidence on how the practice of Islam is detrimental to the black character."* All over the world, Black Muslims are highly known and respected for their strong love and fierce participation in pan-Afrikanism and civil rights movements during freedom struggles. Islam in South Afrika pre-dates the colonial era and more-so the first *Robben Island* prisoners were Muslims, incarcerated by white colonialists in order to prevent them from spreading the religion because, they said, it would teach slaves to rebel.

"During the late seventeenth and early

eighteenth century the Dutch continued to exile Muslim leaders from Batavia to the Cape, they included Sheikh Yusuf of Bantam, who lived at Faure in Cape Town. Probably the first Imam to live in Cape Town was *Said Alochie* of *Mocha* in Yemen, who was sentenced to work on *Robben Island* for ten years in 1747. *Said Alochie* later moved to Cape Town where he worked as a police constable – an occupation which gave him ample opportunities for visiting slave quarters at night and teach.

In 1767 *Prince Abdullah Kadi Abu Salaam of Tidore* was exiled to the Cape. He wrote a copy of the Koran from memory, and the volume is still preserved in Cape Town; *Abdullah* assumed leadership of the community in Cape Town and became known as *"Tuan Guru"*

Islam was a popular religion among the slaves – its tradition of teaching enabled literate slaves to gain better positions in their master's households, and the religion taught its followers to treat their own slaves well."

To non-Muslims this act may seem outstanding and amazing, however, in the Muslim world, children plus-minus ten years of age know the whole *Book* by heart, as do many adults. This Holy Book is preserved in the hearts of Muslims around the world, young and old, male and female, rich and poor. But if your heart is filled with words and no action, then you have not learnt anything from the Koran.

Since Islam has re-visited South Afrika, countless Blacks are reverting each day; Lonke Udumo Luya Ku Mvelinqangi.

"According to converts quoted by the Christian Science Monitor, their biggest reason for the dramatic rise in Islam is that the religion is a refuge from sex, AIDS, alcoholism, and domestic violence that is rampant in the black townships, where the greatest rates of conversions are seen. It is estimated that Islam is the largest religion of conversion in South

Africa."

"According to Michael Mumisa, a researcher and writer on African Islam, there has been an increase in the number of black South Africans converting to Islam particularly among the women and the youth. He believes that for some of the youth and women who were schooled in the politics of South African resistance and confrontation with the security forces of the former Apartheid state, the acceptance of Islam has become part of radical rejection of a society based on Christian principles which are seen as having been responsible for establishing and promoting the Apartheid doctrine through the Dutch Reformed Church in South Africa."

There are those who have been saying that Islam was silent in the South Afrikan struggle. They are ignorant of the facts; they did not do their research right, if they did it at all.

Mahatma Gandhi, a Hindu apologist, regarding South Afrikan Apartheid struggle and Islam, said; *"Someone has said that Europeans in South Africa dread the advent of Islam – Islam, that civilized Spain; Islam that took the torch of light to Morocco and preached to the world the Gospel of Brotherhood. The Europeans of South Africa dread the advent of Islam, as they claim equality with the white races. They may well dread it. If brotherhood is a sin, if it is equality of the coloured races that they dread, then their dread is well-founded."*

It was Black, dark-skinned *Moroccans* who ruled and civilized Spain for 800 years. Islam has proved itself to be a call to unity, call to Black consciousness and racial pride without arrogance, while calling men to their Creator and resisting any kind of oppression, as we would remember *Kunta Kinte*, a Black Muslim from Gambia who resisted slavery in American plantations.

That being said and made clear, I think this would be a good opportunity to address some of the Brothers of ours, those who give poor people food and clothes and then tell them about Islam. This act is anti-Islamic, the Prophet (pbuh) never gave anyone food and then invited them into Islam. If a person came to him hungry, he gave him food and let him leave, and when he preached, he never brought any food or gifts with him. Even though this comes from the goodness and purest of heart, it can be seen as bribery and trickery, because most poor people are now converting in large numbers for the sake of material benefits and not the religion. This act is a very kind act, and it shows concern for mankind, especially the less fortunate, however, if it is done in a wrong way it creates confusion and becomes haraam. Food and clothes are to help poor Muslims and non-Muslims, not for inviting poor people into Islam. This is the sole reason we find every street beggar in 'Islamic clothing' – this is now their begging uniform, it seems. The Prophet of Islam (pbuh) made it clear that *"It is best to give a beggar something or, when not possible, make an excuse with modesty."* However, my beloved Brothers, the distinction between a beggar (someone who seeks to fulfill the bodily need) and a potential revert (someone who seeks spiritual knowledge and fulfillment) must be clearly understood. Another even more important message of warning goes to my South Afrikan *Indian* and *Pakistani* Muslim brothers who treat their

Black employees (Muslim or non-Muslim) like worthless dogs, late-paying them and underpaying them. Does not Islam tell you to pay up your workers his wage before his sweat dries? Therefore you are doing an injustice to Islam for you are giving it a bad name and driving non-believers and non-Muslims even further away from the Religion. This act is anti-Islamic and inhumane therefore I rightfully urge my Black employee Brothers and Sisters to face these tyrant-behaving employers and look them in the eye without any fear and tell them *you are not behaving like a Muslim*, for surely, this act is strongly forbidden in Islam and it will never be tolerated. Islam is perfect, Muslims are not, and wherever we recognize error, we have to correct it by action or by word of advice. These are the same non-black Muslims who disregard Black nationalism because they reject the fact that the 'Black problem' is an isolated problem. These are the same Muslims who glorify Brother *Malcolm X* for wrong reasons.

Islam has always been the Governance that made sense (scientifically, socially, philosophically and spiritually) to the struggling Black man and woman, no wonder the honest mass Black conversion hasn't stopped until this very day. *Koran 9:33: "It is He who has sent His Messenger with guidance and the Governance of Truth, so that He may make it prevail ideologically over every other Governance, however much the polytheists may hate this."* Faith is born of knowledge; faith without knowledge is 'blind faith'. It will not surprise you in learning that Islam places knowledge above faith. *"The inhabitants of the heavens and the Earth and (even) the fish in the deep waters will ask forgiveness for the learned man. The superiority of the learned over the devout is like that of the moon, on the night when it is full, over the rest of the stars" – Sunan of Abu-Darwood, Hadith 1631*

My aim is not to beautify Islam over other religions, which would be a misrepresentation and injustice to Islam itself. The first major step to understanding Islam is realizing that Islam is misunderstood. Islam is the first and last Governance; it is both the foundation and the roof of life on earth. It would be unfair and unrealistic to tell the whole world to believe in this Governance, or to adopt or adapt to Islamic ways. However, for the Black man in South Afrika, rich or poor, learned or illiterate, Islam-*Izimiso Zika*

Mvelinqangi (IsiNtu), may not seem to be the answer, it may not be seductive or glamorous enough but it could solve many of our issues that would heal our sickened condition. But, if it is attraction and glamour that we want, how can the devil fail to entice us and lead us astray? So many questions are running through your head right now; "what about the Arabic language, I can't understand it, and its relevance, do I have to change my name, what is the relevance of this, do I have to change my wardrobe, watch less television, or no television at all, eat halaal (permissible) products only, pray five times a day, what about all the bombing in the so-called Muslim world, all the terrorism, how do I deal with all that, will it concern me when I accept the teachings of Islam?" Yes, all these things and more will concern you, a Muslim never stops learning, especially about his Religion. If you do not learn and research for yourself, you will be misled, the enemies of God work tirelessly day and night inventing new ways of misleading the Sons of God, and once you are misled, your faith will be destroyed, and you will be once again be among the *Walking Dead*.

Regarding name-change, Islam teaches us that in order to raise a child well, three things are required; *1: The child must have a good mother. 2: The child must be given a good name. 3: The child must be taught religion.* My name is a classic example of a good name, a name that is an appraisal to God the Almighty. *Abdul-Malik* is my good name. *Malik* means Master, or King, and *Abdul* means slave or servant, therefore, I am referred to as the servant or slave of the Master (uMvelinqangi – the Almighty God Allah). With a name such as this, how can I forget who I am, whom I am here to serve, and what my position and duty in this world is? Therefore, a Muslim is expected (if he does not have a good name, no matter the language) to carry a name of this nature, surnames are not to be changed, that would be disregarding your own father and distorting your linage. The name changing is not foreign to Black South Afrikans and people of the world. Names such as *John, David, Paul, Jacob, Aaron, Michael*, etc. are all Christian names given to people after Christian conversion after baptism; these are Hebrew and Greek names. After a while, most Black babies were born into Christian homes and were therefore born with these names. In Islam names don't have to be Arabic, this is a misconception, but if you have a bad name such as *Hluphekile* (Poor), *Nkinga* (Trouble) etc., when you accept the teachings of Islam you are required to change it, but if you have a good name such as *Sbusiso* (Blessing), *Sipho/Sphiwe* (Gift/Gifted), *Msizi* (Helper), etc., these are Muslim names. However, our Beloved Prophet (pbuh) stated that the most beloved names to Allah are those that have Praise in them, names that are dedicated to Him. Examples of these names are: *Bonginkosi* (Thank Allah), *Nkosinathi* (Allah is with us), *Musawenkosi* (Allah's Mercy), *Mandle'Nkosi* (Allah's Power), *Dumisani* (Worship Allah), etc. These are Muslim names, these are names of believers, so why change them? You are not Arab, you are Zulu, and if you have a Muslim name in your own language, count yourself blessed. And let your friends and everybody else around you call you by your name in full. The Arabic name will, however, work to your benefit to some extent. As we all know, Arabic is a so-called Islamic language (which is not true for God has no language), and we have Muslims in all parts of the world, therefore, if I visit Japan for instance, and a Japanese Muslim introduces himself by his Japanese name, by the time we finish our conversation I would have forgotten what his name was, but as a Muslim, if it is in the Arabic language, as a unifying factor, I will easily remember it and I will immediately realize he's Muslim or has an Islamic background. This is not in any form subjugation to mainstream Islam, I despise mainstream Islam, for it is horribly flawed; Arabic is our Afrikan language and Islam is our Afrikan traditional religion. However, surnames are not to be changed. Every Muslim is required to keep the name of his father. Our Prophet (pbuh) said: *"whoever abandons the name of his father is not one of us"*. The primary reason for this is that in Islam, Nasab (lineage) is to be preserved by all means. If our lineage were to be thoroughly preserved, we could all trace our lineage right back to Adam (pbuh) and even beyond, and to other Prophets also, for example the *Sithole* tribe came from *Job* of the Bible, and the *Gumede* tribe from *John the Baptist*, known in the Koran as *Yahya* (Yeyeye). Moreover, Islam teaches us that every child has the right to know who his/her father is, even an 'adopted child' must remain with the name of his/her biological father. However, in Islam, a child born out of wedlock cannot take the name of his biological father, in fact, Islamic Law does not even recognize him as the father of that child at all; he has no right to that child whatsoever – that child is not his. Isn't this our Afrikan Traditional Religion? Yes it is. In the Afrikan Tradition, a man cannot claim the child if he's not married to the mother until he pays a certain amount of price for the 'damage' as compensation. Islam is nowhere in contradiction with our pure African Traditional lifestyle which we call IsiNtu.

The Black Muslim should not be discouraged or intimidated by the Arabic language, it is one of Afrika's ancient languages. Even Swahili comes from Arabic and Hausa, and above all, it is the language in which the holy – the Final – Revelation, i.e. Koran was revealed. Some scholars claim that the name 'Shaka' (the most known and first leader of the Zulu nation) is rooted in the word 'Shaikh', which, in the Arabic language means 'leader'.

The so-called Middle East is part of Afrika and was first ruled and civilized by original Arabs – dark-skinned Black Arabs. It was, at some point, ruled from Kemet (Egypt). If you read our Bible you will not find anywhere where it claims that *Mary* (may Allah be pleased with her), when she escaped with baby *Jesus* (peace and blessings be upon him) from *Bethlehem* to *Egypt* crossed any ocean or large river, this is because they walked all the way. Our understanding of the holy scriptures becomes lost in translation. For example, look what happened with the Bible after it was translated into different languages, especially English; half the message was lost and twisted in translation such as the word *"US"*, which is used from the beginning of the bible throughout. If you ask a Jew, he will tell you that in his holy Book, the Torah, there is also the word *"US"*, if you go to a Muslim, he will also assure you that in the Koran, there is also the word *"US"*. However, the Jew and the Muslim do not believe in so-called Holy Trinity, but why is this? According to some religious scholars, the Hebrew language and the Arabic language both have *plural of numbers* and *plural of honor*, and these plurals are not the same – the Englishman did not know this; in his language there is no such thing as *plural of honor*, only the *plural of numbers*. In the reality of the revelation the words *"Us"*, *"We"*, *"Our"* are the *plurals of honor* – Supreme God is too great to refer to Himself as *"I"*. There are countless lost meanings due to translations. In his book *What Is His Name? Sheikh Ahmed Deedat* reveals the proper name that Jesus (pbuh) used when referring to God. Under the Chapter: *From The Lips Of Jesus*, he writes: I ask my Christian visitors, "Do you remember your Gospel narrative, that when Christ was supposed to have been on the cross, he cried out with a loud voice:

"ELOI, ELOI LAMA SABACHTHANI? Which is, being interpreted, *My God, My God, why hast thou forsaken me?"* (Mark 15:34)

The above is a translation from the Greek manuscripts "ACCORDING TO ST. MARK." Obviously his Hebrew has a Greek accent. Because, his so-called originals were written in Greek. But listen to Matthew, who is supposed to have written his Gospel originally in Hebrew, which was aimed at the Jews. St. Jerome, an early Christian father of the 4th and 5th centuries after Christ, testifies as follows:

"MATTHEW, WHO IS ALSO LEVI, AND WHO FROM A PUBLICAN CAME TO BE AN APOSTLE, FIRST OF ALL THE EVANGELISTS, COMPOSED A GOSPEL OF CHRIST IN JUDEA *IN THE HEBREW LANGUAGE AND CHARACTERS,* FOR THE BENEFIT OF THOSE OF THE

CIRCUMSISION WHO HAVE BELIEVED."

Naturally, Matthew's accent would be more Semitic (Hebrew and Arabic) than that of Mark. Matthew records the same scene as Mark 15:34, but note the variation of the dialect: *Jesus cried with a loud voice, saying ELI, ELI, LAMA SABACHTHANI? That is to say, My God, My God, why hast thou forsaken me?* (Matthew 27:46).

Please memorize the words – *"Eli, Eli lama sabachthani."* (Eli – pronounced like L and I in English). Utter the words – ELI, ELI, LAMA SABACHTHANI, to your Christian friends and neighbors and ask them whether these words – "Eli, Eli," sounds like "Jehovah, Jehovah!" to them? No! is the answer if they are not deaf. Ask further, whether "Eli, Eli," sounds like "Abba, Abba!" (meaning father, father! In Hebrew) to them? Again the reply will be "No!" if they are not deaf. Can't they see that the cry is to Allah? "Eli, Eli – Elah, Elah, Allah, Allah!" Let them hear these words from your lips and watch their reactions. No honest person can help agreeing with you.

In the same book, Sheikh Ahmed Deedat explains further, recapturing the lost meaning of the word ALLELUYA! He writes:

Now ask your Christian friend, if he had heard the word *"ALLELUYA."* No Christian worth the name will fail to recognize it. Whenever the Christian goes into ecstasy, he exclaims – "Alleluya! Alleluya!", just as we as Muslims might exclaim the *Takbir* – "Allahu Akbar! Allahu Akbar!" Ask him, what is Alleluya? Take him to the Book of Revelation, the last book of the New Testament, Chapter 19; we are informed that there John the disciple of Jesus, saw a vision, in which he heard the angels in heaven singing, Alleluya, Alleluya. He continues: The last syllable "YA" is a vocative and an exclamatory particle in both Arabic and Hebrew meaning "OH!" In other words YA = OH, (the vocative); and YA = (!), a note of exclamation, or an exclamatory particle, or as is more commonly known an exclamation mark.

The Semite, both Arab and Jew, begins with the exclamatory particle or exclamation mark. The Westerner, in his language ends with the exclamatory particle or exclamation mark, e.g. Stop! Go! Fire! Bang!

Let us repeat the above *Tasbih* (words of praise) as an Arab or a Jew: ALLE-LU-YA will be YA-ALLE-LU because, as explained above, YA is always in the beginning in both Arabic and Hebrew. YA ALLE LU would be YA ALLA HU: Meaning, "OH ALLAH!" (You are the Only Being Who deserves worship and Praise) "OH ALLAH!" (You are the Only Being Who deserves worship and Praise).

These are but a few results of changing the language and translating the scriptures. God is the God of all languages, He hears our prayers no matter the language, He does not need our help, therefore, this is to help yourself in understanding His Word accurately.

The European Jesus whom we have been brought up to worship and pray to is a big lie, he is one of the white man's genius creations to make you obey him. Some of you might dislike the idea that you will now have to prostrate when praying, meaning to fall with your face on the ground. But who said there is another praying position? There is no other, because every Prophet of Allah (pbut) prayed in this position, in *Genesis 17:3, Abraham* (pbuh) *"...fell face down in the dust"*, in *Numbers 20:6, Moses* and *Aaron* (pbut) *"...fell on their faces"*. *Elijah* (pbuh) did the same in *1 Kings 18:42*, so did *Jesus* (pbuh) in *Matthew 26:39*, and many other prophets before him, such as *David* and *Joshua* (pbut) in *1 Samuel 20:41* and *Joshua 5:14. Numbers 16:22*, and *Joshua 7:6* adds to this fact. If this was the way of your Prophets (pbut), then who gave authority as to change this prayer posture? If this was their way, as God commanded, it is our way as well. In fact, almost all, if not every gesture or stance of the Muslim prayer can be traced from the bible for point of reference – from the taking off of the shoes when entering the Mosque (holy ground) which is in *Exodus 3, verse 4-5*, where God orders *Moses* (pbuh) to take his shoes off whenever stepping into His presence; the washing or cleansing of one's certain body parts before prayer can be referred to *Exodus 30, verse 17-21*, as God instructed *Aaron* (pbuh), and praying facing in the direction of the Kabba (Sacred Mosque) as how Christians were required to pray facing in the direction of Jerusalem when making their prayers three times a day during prescribed times, *Daniel 6:10*, and right up to praying with our hands open rather than closed, just as *King Solomon* (pbuh) did *"...with his hands spread up to heaven"*, *1 Kings 8:54*. As Muslims this is what we do for *Solomon*, for *Moses* and *Aaron* (pbut), we make *Qubanni* (sacrifice) for *Abraham* (pbuh).

Islam respects *Jesus, Moses*, and all other prophets, going an extra mile by adding the "Peace Be Upon him" utterance when mentioning their names. Other Black Brothers and Sisters might complain about the 'Islamic' clothing, also attributing it to a foreign culture. In a book titled *The Relevant History of Mankind* by *Nathan Schur*, I quote: *"Egypt was never as fully urbanized as Mesopotamia or classical Greece. Dresses changed, from simple white garments to multi-coloured ones, woven on more sophisticated looms."* Does not this sound like robes worn by Afrikans all over the Afrikan continent? If it was worn in ancient Afrika how is it foreign to you? Does this kind of clothing not protect women from being judged and harassed for how they look? This is our way of clothing, it has always been, and there is no such thing as 'Islamic clothing' – Muslims are to cover their bodies in a modest form. Prophet Muhammad (pbuh) made a certain prayer whenever wearing a new garment, he said: *"O Allah, all praises are due to You Alone. You have given me this garment to wear. I ask You the goodness of this garment and the goodness of that for which it is made and I ask Your Protection from the evil of this garment and the evil of that for which it can be used"* (Tirmidhi). With a prayer such as this, who can, in his/her right mind, leave the house looking indecent? It is Westernization that continuously proves itself to be godless, the kind of system that narrows his thinking ability, corrupts his mind, and fills his tongue with filth, and then gives him 'freedom of speech'. Isn't this hypocrisy? We stare at ignorance in the face and we call it wisdom, greed we call success, envy we call (healthy) competition, and tragically, death we call life.

The Black non-Muslim woman is struggling with the thought of having to wear *hijab* (head scarf) at all times. But what is the problem, really! What is the fuss all about? I ask myself: is not the Black woman (traditionally) obliged to cover her hair? Isn't this a symbol of self-respect and dignity in our tradition and culture? Why do the 'urbanized' Black woman treat this practice as a foreign phenomenon? Are we so caught up and bought into 'white' ways that we can't even remember who we are and what is ours? *Carol Ralefeta, my Black Sister* wrote: *"I can't help but think, we as black women look after our weaves better than our natural hair. Should it not be other way around? After all, natural hair is priceless, it's God-given."* She adds: *"With all the chemicals and hair extensions we put in our hair, it's inevitable that at some point our hair will give in"* (taken from SOUL magazine, November 2011, page 61). Now who can say nurturing and keeping your hair natural, as it was created by the Creator is not part of God-worship. The world associates natural hair (God's creation; God's gift) with filth and untidiness, instead our Black Sisters prefer 'Brazilian (natural) hair' or 'Indian (natural) hair', or 'White (natural) hair', or 'Whatever (natural) hair' but their own. Why is the Church allowing any deviation of God-worship such as this act to take place even inside the church itself (which is the House of Worship)? The corrupted minds call it *'Freedom of Expression'*, and *'Freedom of Choice'*, and the righteous minds call it Self-Rejection, rebellion against God's Will. Simplicity keeps you productive and fruitful; sophistication makes you unproductive and lazy. From one look at a woman's hands, you can tell whether she is busy or lazy, whether she's hands-on or hands-off. With all the fancy manicures and hairstyles that women wear today, they keep them from doing work, whether domestic or industrial. Today, the Black woman, young and old, wears skimpy outfits, bares her body to strangers, and justifies it by claiming this act to be *African*. They say it's the way of the Zulus to bare flesh. If this is so, they should walk bare-foot as well, they should speak only the indigenous language, and remain domesticated. Instead, showing off her body seem to be the only 'Zulu' thing she's dedicated to; then after, she uploads her skimpy sex-orientated pictures onto various social networks in order to be rated and voted for, begging for acceptance and prostituting herself for compliments. It is critical to examine where this need for acceptance and lust for appraisal comes from. God the Almighty created you the way you are therefore He accepts you as you naturally are, and if God the All Mighty accepts you, is there any greater acceptance out there? If you believe there is then you are an idolater, and you've been used as Satan's instrument to stir up unneeded sexual urges amongst the opposite sex. Remember, the audience that accepts you today will tomorrow reject you, and the admirers that compliment you today will tomorrow criticize you.

From *The Sayings of Rumi and Iqbal*, I would like to share a poem titled *The Misled Woman*, which describes this very woman, who I believe is not *Bad* or *Evil*, but merely misled .

> There is that childless, delicate looking woman;
> her bewitching glances give birth to upheaval thoughts
> and receives light from the fire of the West.
> Her appearance is that of a woman, her inner self is unwomanly.
> Her freedom lacks modesty and gives rise to mischief.
> Her "Freedom" is unaware of modesty and shame.
> It would be better if such a flower were never to be born in our garden.
> It would be better if this stigma were washed clean from the dress of the community.

From the same book, the poets blessed us with a very beautiful poem I will only share parts of called *An Address To Muslim Women*, who obviously is the opposite of the misled woman:

> Your chaste nature is blessing for us.
> It is the strength of our faith and foundation of our community.
> Your affection moulds our behavior and conduct,
> our thoughts, our talk, and our actions.
> The present age is full of deceit and cunning;
> its caravan is the robber of the wealth of the faith.
> Its prey calls itself free and the one killed by it,
> regards himself alive.
> Beware of the robbery of these times and hold your children close to your bosom.
> These garden birds that have not yet unfolded their wings,
> have fallen far away from their nest.
> It is the flame from which sparks have spread out,
> and without whose fire the soul and the body could not have acquired a unified form.

It is from her worthiness that we have achieved worth;

it is through her formative contribution that we are what we are.

If God has granted you the light of the eye, purify yourself and see her divine personality.

Man's lyre acquires melody from music produced by woman.

It is her humility that feeds man's vanity.

Woman is the dress that covers man's nakedness.

The heart searching beauty is the dress of love.

The Muslim who regards the woman as mere servant, has not benefited at all from the wisdom of the Quran.

Woman's affection is like the affection of the Prophet of God.

It shapes the character of the nations.

Most so-called non-Muslim Black people, when asking me about Islam they would want to know where does the Muslim stand with the concept of God, and this is the most important question for every religion, and there are those who would ask me, some out of curiosity and others out of sarcasm, whether it is true that the Muslim uses his hand and water after relieving himself in the toilet – and we shall answer both questions as clearly as we possibly can.

What is the Muslim's stand regarding the concept of God? The Muslim is the believer in One God whom he calls Allah (God the All Mighty, Creator of Heaven and Earth in the Arabic language). This God is the Creator of all that exists, the seen and the unseen. He created Heavens and Earth and all of humanity, and all that exists in it. He is the very same God of Adam, Noah, Abraham, Moses, Jesus, Muhammad (pbut), and all other Prophets and Messengers that touched the earth, known and unknown. He is One, He has no partner or assistant, He has no family, i.e. children or spouse or parents and He has no gender. He is Alone and He is Almighty. When the Muslim prays, he prays to Him directly, not via any so-called intermediary, not via Prophet Muhammad (pbuh), not via the *Kaaba*, nor via anything nor anybody but Him directly, and this shall bring us to our next question. If God was standing right before you, facing you, listening to you talking to Him, and you can see Him, would you allow yourself to face Him unclean or smelling funny? Obviously not. Now imagine: He's not in front of you, He's within you. And since the Muslim prays or talks to God directly as though he sees Him, he is required to wash his mouth, removing any dirt from food particle remains and killing any taste of whatever he last ate, leaving him with the pure natural taste of clean water, and rinsing his nose, washing his face and arms and legs, and cover himself well, and with clean clothes – if possible. If he has had sexual intercourse, he is required to wash his whole body ritualistically in running water before standing 'before' the Almighty God. Cleanliness is an Islamic practice, not just a prayer ritual. A Muslim is required to stay clean at all times, as the Koran says in 74:1 *"O, you wrapped in your cloak, arise and give warning! Proclaim the glory of your Lord; purify your garments; shun uncleanness."*

Prophets of God the Almighty did not teach about anything before teaching about *Cleanliness* (Inhlanzeko). Inhlanzeko is the foundation of Ukholo and the foundation of nation building. It is divided in three parts, as my teacher *The Honorable Minister Adam T. Mbhele Ka Ncanywa* taught me; 1) Physical, 2) Mental, 3) Spiritual Cleanliness. Man should strive to remain clean in all these three aspects because Man is God of the universe. Most important aspects of physical cleanliness is washing your behind thoroughly with water after relieving yourself. Water removes every dirt, germ, and smell. Rinse your mouth after meals; food remains causes bad breath and rotten teeth. And circumcise, for circumcision reduces sensitivity and reduces the risks of UTI (Urinary Tract Infection) and other infections. Therefore, since water kills all dirt and gems and kills smell, there is nothing better than water to use after relieving yourself. This is exactly why we wash our hands before we eat, this is why we bath; we do not wipe our bodies with paper and go to work, we use water, water kills gems and smell and it refreshes and cools the body. This is how our ancestors did it, and moreover using the left hand *(Isandla sekhohlo/Inxele)*. This is the hand they used for wiping their behind after relief, not the right hand because the right hand is *Isandla Sokudla*. Some of you, the so-called civilized, laugh at this practice but your very own civilization does not. Modern civilization has said that it is better, cleaner and hygienic for you to wipe your behind or hands using newly invented wet wipes rather than dry wipes; and one does not need a brain to figure out that water itself cleans even better than wet wipes, therefore, in near future prepare that you will be advised to use water, which is what cleans thoroughly, and when that day comes, do not forget to give credit where it is due.

Have you noticed how white people eat, have you? Have you noticed that they use a fork and a knife. Have you noticed that you, also, my Black, Indian, and Coloured Brothers, have adopted this practice? Have you noticed that you see this practice as etiquette? My poor beloved Brothers, I bet you never noticed that when you eat this way you hold your fork and eat with your Left hand, the hand made for toilet use. They told you these are 'Table Manners', while their table is filled with stinking toilet habits. My dear Brothers, never again laugh at what you do not understand – many a time you will find that the joke is on you. While we've just dealt with the subject of food and how to eat, we might as well follow it with the subject of *ukudla okuvumelekile* (Halaal foods), which is a great taboo and misunderstood amongst my Black South African Brothers. The word 'halaal' simply means 'permissible' or 'allowed', it's the opposite of the word 'haraam', which means 'impermissible'. These words are not just restricted to food only, but also to the way a decent human being speaks, the way he dresses, walks, etc. My 'non-Muslim' Brothers and Sisters wonder in awe as to why Muslims over stress about whether the restaurant serves halaal foods or not. When our Afrikan ancestors had to slaughter an animal they would feed it well and give it water to drink, and keep away from it while keeping tools used for slaughter out of it sight. They would first ask for permission from uMvelinqangi, Supreme Owner of all that is on earth and in Heavens. They would say,"*eGameni lika Mvelinqangi, uMvelinqangi uPhakame*". Then they would find a very sharp knife to cut the animal with (not stab). The slaughtered animal mustn't feel pain and go through shock for two reasons; mercy, and the fact that when you are in a state of shock and anxiety your system releases toxic chemical juices which are poisonous – they are the biggest cause of diseases. If we do not follow these guidelines then we have not only stolen Gods' creature, but also violated it and caused it pain and horror. The Koran says that it is God Who created the animal. He is the One Who created grass for it to graze upon, and sends down rain for the grass to grow. And yet, when we slaughter that very same animal, we do not mention His Blessed Name, and even worse we mention names of other creations – names of our ancestors or other deities. What an insult this is to Mvelinqangi. Therefore, it is haraam for any Believing men and women to consume meat that was slaughtered for idols without mentioning the Name of God upon it. Another haraam aspect of meat eating is that a Believer is not allowed to eat meat from an animal that was found dead, either by physical harm or disease. These are a few aspects of "halaal" and "haraam", and we, the Bantu people share these aspects with the religion of the Jews, this is what they call "Kosher", which makes it permissible to buy and eat meat from a Jewish shop. And for the record, as Christians as well we were ordered by the Creator to consume clean foods and avoid what my Teacher calls *Ukudla Kwa Sathane*, as we will see in the Koran verse further down.

It would be an absolute lie to say that in the Islamic world, among Muslims, there is perfect *Mahnaj* (Brotherhood) and there is no racism and classism, and any other form of discrimination. In South Afrika, in particular, some members of Indian and Pakistani descent may feel *Islamically* superior to Black Muslims, maybe because they were born into so-called Muslim families (not knowing the Black man is Muslim by nature); therefore, they think that Allah, the Almighty God, is their household pet, and Islam is theirs alone. You see, Black people are sick and tired of white cultural aggression and Indian cultural oppression. Do not be discouraged by these misguided individuals. If they want to talk about skin colour tell them that you, the Black man, is the Original Arab and the Original Hebrew, you are the Original Muslim and the Original Jew. Remind them that all Prophets of Allah were Black, dark-skinned and kinky-haired Afrikans. Tell them that *'Middle-East'* is a Eurocentric term used to mislead us, and the correct term is *"North-East Afrika"* because that is where that land is.

Ninth Century poet named Abu Al Hasan Ali ibn Al-Abbas ibn Jurayj, known to many as Rumi, wrote a long poem to the Abbasids blaming them for the way that they treated the family of Prophet Muhammad (pbuh). It should be understood that at that time, the Abbasids had become very mixed with the settlers (Romans, Greeks, and Persians). Here is part of what Rumi said in his famous poem called *Al-Jeemia*:

"You insulted them (the family of Prophet Muhammad) because of their blackness while they are still pure-blooded black-skinned Arabs. However, you are blue-eyed, the Romans have embellished your faces with their colour."

Now those who secretly hate Black history and work tirelessly distorting it are only left with two choices to choose from; they will either accept that Muhammad (pbuh) was dark-skinned and originally Arab, or light-skinned and not an original Arab.

When lining up for prayer, our beloved *Prophet Muhammad* (pbuh) told us to stand shoulder-to-shoulder, leaving no gap in-between, because, he said, in that gap is where the devil will enter and cause division amongst us. He was referring to the devil called racism, superiority complex and ego. Faithful followers and potential reverts should not be discouraged by witnessing any kind of disunity. If there is no unity, it is not Islam, and those are followers of another governance but not Islam. They may call themselves Muslims; they are misguided. Islam teaches Peace and Unity, even among other faiths and cultures, not hate, especially not amongst fellow Muslims. *"Today, all good things have been made lawful to you. The food of the People of the Book (i.e. Jews and Christians) is lawful to you, and your food is lawful to them. The chaste believing women and the chaste women of the people who were given the Book before you, are lawful to you, provided that you give them their dowers, and marry them, neither committing fornication nor taking them as mistresses."* – 5:5, Holy Koran.

Islam is Perfect, Muslims are *not*. And most people believe in God, the question is what does one follow. The Muslim believes in God and he *follows* Islam. Being a Muslim is easy. A Muslim is one who believes that God is One, like the Zulus did before settlers came with their version of the Bible. The Black man never had crafted any sculptures of God because in his belief there is nothing like Him, He is the

Hidden One, and this is the truest definition of a *Muslim* embodied in an ancient Zulu man. A Muslim is the one who believes that no one is worthy of worship but God, alone, and that there is no one like Him. And Islam is the perfect doctrine that which a Muslim should follow in order to be successful in this world and in the Hereafter.

As people, we want to believe in a religion when we are a hundred percent assured that all its' followers are perfect, then accept that religion as accurate, but this is unrealistic – as much as we have good Muslims, we also have bad Muslims, so are Jews, Atheists, Christians, and Traditionalists.

Tried and tested, Islam is a timeless and universal religion that which teaches men natural laws; in *30:30-32,* the holy Quran states: *"Devote yourself single-mindedly to the Divine Governance. And follow the nature (constitution) as made by God, that nature in which He has created mankind. There is no altering the creation of God. That is the right religion. But most people do not realize it. Turn to Him and fear Him, and be steadfast in prayer, and do not be one of those who associate partners with God, those who split up their religion and become divided into sects;*

each one exulting in what they have."

I tell my Jewish Brother; Islam is Moses' Revelation. I say to my Christian Brother; Islam is Injeel le Issa (Gospel of Jesus), and, if we strip down our Afrikan Tradition, if we remove all the innovations, coatings and decorations and strip it naked, deep down underneath lies Islam (IsiNtu). After all is said and done, after all the complaints and confusions, Allah made everything easy and clear for us in the Holy Koran, and we believe in His Wisdom, and we believe in Him, Alone.

May Allah help us remember Him, may the holy Koran stay a Reminder and Warning, may we remember these words: *"Remember Me when you are rich, I will remember you when you are poor. Remember Me when you are happy, I will remember you when you are sad. Remember Me when you are healthy, I will remember you when you are sick. And remember me when you are alive, and I will remember you when you die".*

I agree with those who say *Love* is the answer to Revolution. But what is Love, and who is the source of Love? The answer is God the Almighty. Therefore, it is only logical that we invite the Almighty God uMvelinqangi and let His Love lead the way and guide us until we revolutionalize ourselves, because that is where true revolution begins – in each of us, whether one is Black or white, Muslim or Christian, ANC or IFP, rich or poor. May God bless us, may He increase in us knowledge, may He save us from Hell Fire and make Paradise our Final dwelling place. Ameen!

May we stay constantly reminded that it's all about *Love* and it's all about the *People*.

We will lead the revolution!

I hope God the Almighty has blessed this union.

I leave you with a Universal Revolutionary Salutation of Peace and Solidarity: As-Salaam Alaikum! Ukuthula Makube Kuwe.

"...but do not think that the awakening I have referred to was something like being "born-again"; I did not have to be reformed from a sinful life to become a Muslim, I was a staunch Christian all my life and I never missed any church service. The awakening I have referred to was a new discovery, a discovery which changed my life, my way of thinking and my general behavior. I suddenly became aware of the purpose for my being and of my duty to God and to men. The things that were of value to me suddenly became valueless and the "pretended happiness" of Christendom became a mockery and a clumsy hand beckoning one to hell.

"For the first time I began to realize what I have to do for the remaining days of my life in order to gain eternal happiness Insha-Allah (God willing). I looked at the wasted sixty-five years of my life and felt the urgency to write and inform those people who like me are sincere in their wish to worship God, the creator of the Heaven and the Earth. People who are prepared to seek the truth and are willing to accept the truth, whatever it may cost. People who believe in life after death, and have a desire to enjoy that eternal life at the end of their earthly days. But more importantly, people who have the guts to change their lives in spite of public opinion.

PUBLIC OPINION PLAYS A MAJOR ROLE IN OUR DAILY ACTIVITIES. SOME PEOPLE HAVE SUFFERED SILENTLY UNDER DIFFICULT CIRCUMSTANCES FOR FEAR OF PUBLIC OPINION, OTHERS HAVE LOST FORTUNES AND OTHERS MAY LOSE THEIR SOULS FOR FEAR OF PUBLIC OPINION."

– Sheikh Dawood Ngwane

Anything good I may have said is from Allah, any mistakes are my own and from Satan, may Allah forgive me. I seek refuge in Allah from giving wrong advice and from all forms of trials and tribulations, AMEEN!

ABOUT THE BOOK

*T*he *Condition of the Black Man* is a five-year project by revolutionary writer and social justice activist Abdul-Malik Masoka, born 33 years ago in the city of Durban, KwaZulu-Natal where he currently lives and works.

As an avid blogger, essayist, author and poetry writer, this work comes as no surprise to close acquaintances; in fact, it has been a long awaited debut, and perhaps a long overdue one.

To sensitive readers, the book may seem full of criticism, but there is a difference between criticism and critical analysis, and this book is based on critical analysis. With socio-political lessons drawn from childhood memories and life-long experience as an observant teenage and an inquisitive young adult, the writer takes a critical look at social ills, attempting to discover the fundamental yet overlooked causes. In addition to examining issues such as the duality of the Black character caused by religious and traditional identities, this book looks at the pre and post Apartheid political reality in South Afrika in the most objective way while it tends to question everything and everyone in question. Overall, this book attempts to bring the Black man back to himself, back to his supreme and noble stature. It attempts to draw important parallels between Islam and IsiNtu, which the writer insists are one-and-the-same Law and Practice. He believes the two practices have been corrupted over time but nevertheless, when one goes deep into their roots one finds the same Supreme and Divine Law. References are Scriptural, primarily Koranic and Biblical, and others by men of Atticism and grand logic and political giants. We honor you all. We stand on your shoulders as we continue the struggle for the emancipation of the Black man.

Look out for future reads by Abdul-Malik Masoka as we soldier-on on this warrior path in the struggle for elevation of the Black mind.

www.ingramcontent.com/pod-product-compliance
Lightning Source LLC
Chambersburg PA
CBHW022103280326
41933CB00007B/245